P9-EKY-890

What's an "A" Anyway?

s: A+ — Excellent, Independent work;
erage; B—Satisfactory Work of Average
s Passing But Can Be Improved; D—
F—Absolute Failure.

Days A...	Deportment	English	Mathematics	Mathematics	Science	Social	Spelling	History	Biology	Biol
									C	a
			a	C					B	B
			B	B					B	B
			B	B						C
			B	C						
			B	C						
5.			B	C						
6.										

What's an "A" Anyway?

HOW IMPORTANT ARE GRADES?

By

MARNI TERKEL

and

SUSAN NEIBURG TERKEL

Franklin Watts
A DIVISION OF SCHOLASTIC INC.
New York • Toronto • London • Auckland • Sydney
Mexico City • New Delhi • Hong Kong
Danbury, Connecticut

To my sister, Alyse Neiburg Blumberg,
who loved school and didn't worry about her grades. S.N.T.
To my best friend, Jason Gardner, who helps me keep my life in
perspective and see both sides of this issue. M.T.

Acknowledgments
The authors would like to thank our editor, Lorna Greenberg, for her astute literary judgment, patience, diligence, and sense of humor. A special thank-you to Howard Pollio, Ph.D., for his advice and encouragement. Much appreciation to Chris Bauer, Blanche Clegg, Debbie Hanger, Elizabeth Franklin, Ted Furman, Brian Garvey, Sarah Honeck, Monica Knooihui-Zen, John Lewis, Sarah Littlefield, Doug Lucas, Chris Mann, Linda Malik, Elaine Portalupi, Margie Smith, Rachel Teumim, and Karen Wood. We are ever so grateful to Dave Terkel for his contributions, as well as to the special men in our lives, Larry Terkel and Jason Gardner.

Photographs ©: AP/Wide World Photos: 47 (Al Behrman), 105 (Karl Deblaker), 53 (M. Spencer Green), 118 (Julia Malakie), 61 (Kathy Willens); Corbis-Bettmann: 76 (Richard Hutchings), 2, 122; Dan Brody: 72 (Packer Collegiate Institute), 51; Eyewire: cover; Impact Visuals/Catherine Smith: 92; Intel Science Talent Search/Mark Portland: 58; Liaison Agency, Inc./J&M Studio: 13; Photo Researchers, NY: 56 (Russell D. Curtis), 89 (Grantpix); PhotoEdit: 87 (Michelle Bridwell), 68 (Mary Kate Denny), 97 (Robert W. Ginn), 111 (Will Hart), 101 (Richard Hutchings), 40 (Phil McCarten), 11, 84 (Michael Newman), 8 (Mark Richards), 16 (D. Young-Wolf); Superstock, Inc.: 19, 22, 24, 27, 33, 37, 43, 70, 79.

Library of Congress Cataloging-in-Publication Data
Terkel, Marni.
    What's an "A" anyway? How important are grades? / by Marni Terkel
and Susan Neiburg Terkel.
        p. cm.
    Includes bibliographic references (p.) and index.
    ISBN 0-531-11417-1
        1. Grading and marking (Students)—United States—Juvenile literature.
    2. Educational tests and measurements—United States—Juvenile literature.
    [1. Grading and marking (Students) 2. Educational tests and measurements.]
    I. Title: How important are grades? II. Terkel, Susan Neiburg.
    III. Title.

LB3051 .T39 2001
371.27'2—dc21   00-043731

Contents

Laying the Foundation

You have just arrived at class after frantically cramming for a big test. Why, oh why, you say to yourself, aren't you better prepared? You wish you had studied more. And you wish grades weren't so important. What's an A anyway? And then you hear those dreaded words, "Okay, everyone. Clear your desks and take out a pencil."

Sickeningly aware of your teacher's footsteps and the knot settling in your stomach, thoughts of "If only . . ." flash before you. "If only I had a few more minutes to study. . . . If only I were sick today. . . . If only the test were tomorrow. . . . If only a genie would arrive and grant me three wishes."

You are brought back to reality by the crinkling of paper as classmates flip over the first page of the test. The scratching of pencils tells you that everyone else is answering questions. Worried about losing time, you are tempted to peek at your neighbor's test. Resisting the urge, you look down—to discover you know the answer to the first question.

"If only the test were tomorrow."

Feeling unprepared or overanxious about a test is an experience many of us know well. So, what can be done about it? Studying more, managing your time better, and improving your learning techniques may help. But sometimes, what you need is a healthier perspective about grades.

Imagine taking this test without grades. Would you be just as nervous? Would you learn the same amount of material? Would there still be a reason to take (or purpose behind) the test?

BACK IN THE OLD DAYS

Do you know what grades Shakespeare received? What about Socrates? Elizabeth I? Benjamin Franklin, Marie Curie, or Jane Austen? Actually, many of the giant figures of our past never received grades. Grades were not introduced until 1783,[1] so before then, no one was graded. Did they receive praise? Most certainly. What about criticism? You bet. Their knowledge was brought into question, evaluated, and assessed. But graded? No, most of them were not graded. But whether graded or not, they were knowledgeable and accomplished.

The root of the word *school* comes from the Greek "schola," meaning leisure. For those of you who dread school, this might be difficult to imagine, but learning in school was a leisure activity that people enjoyed. Of course, some of you find school fulfilling and worthwhile—lucky ducks! Life is just that much easier for you.

FEELING THE PRESSURE

Year after year students are encouraged to get good grades or else . . .

"—you won't be allowed to play on the basketball team."

"—you won't get into a good college."

"—you won't move up in your career."

"—you won't be successful in life."

"—you will be grounded."

The ultimatums vary, but the message is the same: Get good grades and you gain options in life. Get bad grades and you limit your opportunities. Our society sees grades as a ticket to success. Students are told that good grades will earn them a respectable job with a large salary. Some students reap specific awards (cars, trips, honor-roll status) from parents or school administrators for good grades.[2]

Please note: The emphasis is primarily on grades, not learning. Are your parents more concerned with your grades or what you are learning? What do your classmates care more about?

Some of you may have assumed that grades and learning are the same thing—that your grade represents how much you've learned in the class. As you read this book, it will become clear that they may not be the same. For now, think about which question you usually hear after a class test: "How did you do?" (Translation: "Did you know enough to get a good grade?") Or "What was the most thought-provoking question on the test?" (That's what we thought you would say.)

ALL IN ONE

What does it mean to get an A, B, C, D, or F for a paper, test, project, or class? Do your grades say whether you are smart? If you worked hard or learned anything? Whether you are creative and have original thoughts? If you work well with others? Whether you follow directions? Do grades demonstrate that you are compassionate, easy to talk to, and intrigued by new ideas?

Grades are symbols. As symbols, they take on whatever meaning is assigned to them. For example, when a high school student looks at a marked term paper and says "I got a C," he or she means something different from what the preschool child means after picking up an alphabet block and saying "I got a C." Also, C can stand for Celsius, carbon, calorie, a musical note, or the voltage of a battery. The C (or B or F) needs a context in order to have meaning.

But how much can one symbol represent in a context? Can a letter grade represent mastery, effort, creativity, cooperation, intelligence, and critical thinking skills all at once? How does a teacher decide which characteristics to factor

An A—or any other grade—carries whatever meaning is assigned to it.

into a grade and which to leave out? And does a letter grade have a constant meaning, or does each teacher create the meaning for each grade?

FIGURING IT OUT

This book takes you through all of the issues surrounding grades—their meaning, accuracy, importance, purpose, effects, alternatives, and more. By getting the facts, you will have a greater understanding of the role of grades in your life. You will become more informed about grading—what grades can and cannot do, when they are important and when they're not, and how good is good enough. So, come along to explore this complicated and important issue inside and out.

CHAPTER 1

Why Grade?

Believe it or not, grades were not conceived to introduce you to stress, to give your parents something to get on your case about, or to motivate you to work in school. Grading may have yielded these results, but they were not among its original purposes. Let's look at the reasons schools grade today.

GRADES SORT AND RANK

In earlier days, grades were used to compare students and chart their performances. Students were categorized by Latin adjectives—*optimus* (best), second *optimus*, *inferior* (lower), *pejorus* (worse). Later, numerical grades were introduced in an effort to take sorting and ranking to a new level.[1]

Once students began to be graded, those who showed extraordinary aptitude and scholarship could be singled out and acknowledged. That is a pattern we follow today—sorting and ranking students, putting top-graded students on the honor

Grades are used for ranking. The student with the highest grades is often named valedictorian.

roll, and bestowing the honor of being valedictorian on the one who scores highest. Grading also makes it possible to select students who merit academic scholarships.

During the Cold War of the 1950s and 1960s, the United Stated competed with the Soviet Union in science, math, and technology. This race brought ranking and sorting to a new level, as schools decided to "track" their brightest students; placing them in more challenging curricula and classes, including the new advanced placement and honors classes.

GRADES ESTABLISH STANDARDS

A primary purpose of grades is to indicate the level of achievement for a specific period of time. Grades provide a standard that students must meet to move to the next level of study. Students who fail to meet the standard (earn a passing grade) fail the course and may have to repeat it. At the college level, students who fail to meet the standard are not allowed to graduate and, depending on their grades, are put on probation or asked to leave school.

GRADES ARE SHORT AND TO THE POINT

Grades convey information quickly. They are easy to use—for teachers, students, and parents. (It sure doesn't take parents long to read a report card!) In fact, opponents of grades argue that grades do not help students learn but only help the school keep track of how each student is doing.[2]

GRADES INFORM ABOUT STUDENTS' WORK

Grades let you, and those who care about you, know how you are doing in school. Theoretically, if you are responsible, well organized, and put forth some effort, you will receive good grades. If you neglect to do homework or hand in assignments, don't pay attention, and take an "I don't care" attitude, your grades will be lower. Good grades signal that you are doing okay; bad grades signal that you need help.

GRADES HELP YOU PRIORITIZE

Suppose that tomorrow you have a project due in American history. It is to include a written report and a visual component, each worth a zillion points. You also have a math assignment due, which will count for only a small percentage of your final math grade but will take a lot of time. You also face an English quiz. How do you allocate your time? How much will your concern about grades affect your decision (as opposed to, say, what you really want to learn or think is important to know)?

Here's another example. Suppose that you are rockin' out with an A in earth science and an A+ in French. You have a B in American government and a B- in English literature. In geometry, you are on the verge of failing. Which subject will you give the most attention? To avoid summer school, you'll need to spend the most time on your least-favorite subject.

GRADES HOLD STUDENTS ACCOUNTABLE

Before students were graded, there was no reason for teachers to give tests. Can you imagine never taking tests? Many teachers, however, welcome tests because they make the students more responsible for learning.

Grades allow teachers to evaluate students without bringing their own opinions into the evaluation. So when a student gets a poor grade and the student, the parents, or the school administration want to know why, the teacher can open a handy-dandy grade book and an explanation appears: "Johnny received a D because he scored poorly on this test, he failed this quiz, and his paper was shorter than assigned and filled with grammatical errors."

GRADES ARE USEFUL FOR COLLEGE ADMISSIONS OFFICES

Some colleges admit any student with a high school diploma or a GED (a high school equivalency degree you can earn by passing standardized tests in various subject areas). Other institutions are more selective. Although grades are not the only factor considered for admission, with thousands of applications to weed through, college admissions offices find grades and class rank useful. Whenever colleges face a surge in applications, the emphasis on high school grades and class rank increases significantly.

After World War II, the U.S. government passed the GI bill, by which the government undertook to pay the tuition of veterans who wanted to attend college or graduate school. The schools were flooded with applications. Grade point averages (GPAs), class rank, and SAT exams gained importance.

A generation later, the huge postwar cohort of baby

From gold stars to banners and badges, schools offer an array of awards for high grades.

boomers was competing for college admission—again increasing the importance of grades and class rank. In recent years, the thriving economy has enabled high school seniors to apply to many colleges. In the past, they might have been hampered by the cost of multiple applications. Yet again, the emphasis on grades and class rank increased.

GRADES SERVE AS REWARDS AND PUNISHMENTS

Many people believe that grades motivate students to study and try to do well. As one teacher stated, "Grades are necessary because without them my students wouldn't do their work." It is not surprising that teachers draw this conclusion. Think of how often they are asked, "Will this be graded?" or "Will we need to know that for the test?"

Clearly, there are reasons for grades. Next step: let's grade the grades.

CHAPTER 2

What Do Grades Tell Us?

What does a C mean?

To students, a grade of C can mean:

"Average, whatever that is."

"I was bored and didn't pay attention."

"My parents will ground me."

"That I'm not good at the subject."

"That I studied and did well for once."

"That I didn't try hard."

"If I hadn't cheated, I would have gotten an F."

"Depends on who the teacher is."

To parents, a C says:

"Ruth needs to study more."

"The class is too hard."

"Eric needs a tutor."

"Shawn is a slow reader and everything takes so long!"

"Carl will be okay. I got C's but an A in social skills."

"Alan needs new friends; his crowd is corrupting him."

"A C! I wish my daughter brought home C's."

To teachers, a C says:

"The student didn't do what I asked."

"It depends on the assignment."

"The content was great, but the spelling and punctuation were horrendous."

"It depends on who gets the C."

"A's on tests with incomplete homework calculate to a final grade of C."

"The student didn't grasp the concept, didn't show the work, or made careless mistakes."

There you have it: A grade means something different for everyone and in every situation. Some students are thrilled to get a C, while others are disappointed. Some care about their grades, some don't; and some wish they didn't have to care but their parents pressure them. Some students work hard for C's, others get C's with little effort.

Where do you fall into this picture? Are you excited, satisfied, or disappointed with a C? Does it depend on the class or assignment, or is your reaction always the same? Finally, do you view your grades the same way you view other students' grades?

Students' views of grades are influenced by:

Expectations and goals

Past performances

Effort expended

Parents' attitudes

Are you satisfied or disappointed with a C?

Interest in material
Life situation
Views of teachers' grading style
College plans

Parents' views of grades are influenced by:
Child's age or grade level
Difficulty of the class or test
Reputation of school
Child's past grades
Views of child's potential
Thoughts about child's future
Friends' children's grades
Personal experience with grades
Experience with college
Profession

A school's view of grades depends on:
School's mission statement
Student population

Grading scale
Principal's background with grades
Teachers' views of assessment

Teachers base their views of grades on:
Expectations for students
Information and skills they value
Style of teaching
Experiences in the classroom
Views of education

Just as some students care about grades while others do not, some teachers think grades are necessary while others think they interfere with the learning process.

DON'T JUDGE A BOOK BY ITS COVER

Let's say you bring home mostly C's and your older brother earned all A's and B's. Do these grades tell your parents anything about the type of student you and your brother are? What if your classes are harder, or your teachers are tougher graders? Let's look at how teachers feel about this issue.

Twenty-two teachers were asked, "What does a B mean?" Their answers varied but most were straightforward and clear about their grading policies. Later, these teachers were told that their own child received a C in a college course. Interestingly, when a family member got the C, the majority of teachers felt they needed more information before they could say what it meant.[1] If these teachers couldn't explain what a grade meant unless they knew more about the context, why do other people think they can?

20

VARIATION AMONG THE SCALES

Schools that grade typically use one of three grading scales. (Funny that there's not a universal scale!) Sometimes a school uses a more lenient scale for advanced courses and a tougher scale for regular courses.

Letter Grades	Numerical Range[2]		
	School 1	School 2	School 3
A	90–100	93–100	95–100
B	80–89	85–92	88–94
C	70–79	77–84	81–87
D	60–69	69–76	75–80
F	0–59	0–68	0–74

Look at these three scales closely. Depending on which scale your school uses, an 80 percent could earn a B (school 1), a C (school 2), or a D (school 3).[3]

Now think about this: A grade of B has a range of 9 to 12 points, depending on the school, but the difference between a B and a C is always just one point. Even with the easiest grading scale, there are 59 point possibilities for an F and only 10 for every other grade.[4] The odds aren't in your favor!

TESTS MAKE A DIFFERENCE

Chances are test grades will make up a large part of your final grade in a class. But what material is on the tests, how the tests are formatted, and how they are graded will all affect your test grades. And while your understanding of the material will probably be most important, your teacher and his or her mood and values may factor into the final result.

Content. Some teachers base tests on class discussions or lectures. Others test straight from the textbook. Some want you to recall basic facts. Others test you on how well you apply the material to a situation. Some teachers spell out what you'll need to know in advance, while others leave it a mystery.

Format. Teachers choose from a variety of test types: multiple-choice, true/false, matching, fill-in-the-blank, short answer, essay.

Studies show that students who care about their grades often prefer multiple-choice or matching tests because it is easier to make educated guesses with these formats. Students who care about learning and don't pay as much

A test can challenge a student to apply what has been taught.

attention to their grades prefer essay tests, since they give the test takers a chance to explain their answers and show what they've learned. No students thought multiple-choice tests helped them learn, but many believed essay tests did help them learn and remember the information.[5]

Grading the test. Does your teacher give partial credit when you miss a detail but get part of the answer correct, or does he or she have an all-or-nothing attitude? Do your history tests seem like English tests too, because the teacher takes off points for misspelled words and grammatical mistakes? And does your math teacher take off points if you don't show all your work?

VEGETABLE STEW

If you look up vegetable stew in five cookbooks, chances are each cookbook will have a different recipe and each author will consider his or hers the best. Just as each cook chooses which vegetables to include in a stew, each teacher selects the ingredients to make up grades and how much of each ingredient to use. For example, when grading a paper or project, one teacher might accept work no matter how late it is; another may deduct points for each late day; yet another teacher may not accept any late work, even for partial credit.

Teachers usually spell out their expectations on what will be graded. However, once a final grade is on the student's report card, only the teacher knows what ingredients went into it. Even when teachers use similar recipes for grading, their grades can mean different things. No two teachers teach in the same manner. Not all teachers are equally gifted. Most teachers do the best they can, but sometimes their ability or their knowledge of the subject matter may fall short. You may sometimes have an imperfect teacher—and you may have to make the best of it.

A generic recipe for a course grade

Mastery of the class material

Test and quiz scores

Quality and performance of assignments

Ability to reason and think critically

Classroom participation

Effort

The teacher decides which ingredients make a grade

Preparation for class
Attitude and work ethic
Study skills and habits
Potential
Behavior
Attendance and tardiness
Compliance with directions
Neatness

GRADING IS NOT AN EXACT SCIENCE

With today's standardized tests and classroom requirements, teachers are generally told precisely what to teach and sometimes even when to teach it. However, when it comes to grading, teachers still have a tremendous amount of freedom.

Few school systems encourage teachers to use the same standards and practices for grading—except for the use of a uniform grading scale. So anyone outside the class is not aware of how a teacher grades and therefore cannot accurately interpret a grade. Do people want to admit this? Some will, but many people aren't even aware it is a concern.

While some schools across the country are reevaluating their grading practices, many are not. And often the work of examining and challenging grading policies is at an early stage. As an example, one school is encouraging teachers to share and analyze student work (without disclosing the students' or teachers' names) as a basis for developing grading guidelines. The vice-principal of the school hopes the process will help new teachers develop grading policies and encourage veteran teachers to coordinate their practices.

Progress may come from these efforts, yet teachers are still ultimately free to grade however they want. The grades will continue to mean little outside of the school walls. Does this mean grades are useless? We are not going that far. But we should acknowledge that grades are often subjective, affected by chance, and easily misinterpreted. With this understanding, grades can serve their purposes.

CHAPTER 3

Putting Grades to the Test: How Reliable Are They?

O kay, pop quiz time! Don't worry—we know you haven't finished reading this book. This brainteaser will get you thinking about how trustworthy grades really are (or aren't) and will illustrate some of the decisions teachers have to make when grading.

To begin, find some paper and a pencil. Have fun, and good luck! (Since one purpose of a test is to give feedback about what you need to work on, the answer key, with explanations, appears after the test.)

True/False section: Number your paper from 1 to 4. Determine whether the following four statements are true or false. Write "True" or "False" next to each number. Be prepared to explain your answer, and DO NOT write on the test itself (unless you own the book)!

If everyone in the class masters the material, will everyone get an A?

1. If everyone in a class masters the material and adequately meets the teacher's expectations, the teacher will give everyone in the class an A.
2. If two teachers teach the same course, use the same textbook, assign the same homework, and give the same tests, students who perform equally will earn the same grade.
3. Grading scales are subject to change at the teacher's discretion.
4. An F on a transcript is worse than not having taken the course.

Multiple-choice section: Skip a line and number your paper from 5 to 8. Each question starts with a statement or question that refers to a teacher's dilemma. Read the choices carefully, then select the most appropriate answer. Write the letter of your answer choice next to the corresponding number on your paper.

5. What should a teacher do when a student does not meet a deadline?

   a. The teacher should grade the assignment as if it had been turned in on time. It is more important for a student to do the work well than to turn it in on a specific day.

   b. The teacher should accept the assignment but take off points for every late day. Otherwise, it isn't fair to the students who worked hard to meet the deadline.

   c. The teacher should accept the late assignment and give the student feedback, but he or she should assign the student a grade of zero. Welcome to the real world. What do you think happens to lawyers who miss a filing deadline? They can be sued.

6. A teacher gives a test with two essay questions. One student writes only one essay. That essay, however, is well thought out, well written, and the best essay of the class. How should the teacher grade the test?[1]

   a. The teacher should give the student an A, since that is the grade the essay deserves.

   b. The teacher should give the student a B, since the essay showed mastery of the subject matter and an ability to apply the material. The student does not deserve an A, because of the failure to follow directions.

   c. The teacher should calculate the test using the point system. Give the student the maximum number of points for the first essay, and a zero for the second essay question and then average the two scores.

   d. The teacher must assess whether the student skipped the second essay by mistake or on purpose. Did the student need more time, misread the directions, or not know the answer?

7. A student writes an F paper.
   a. An F paper deserves an F.
   b. The student should have the opportunity to rewrite the paper, and the two grades should be averaged.
   c. The student should be given a chance to rewrite the paper, and the new grade should replace the F.
   d. The student should drop out of the class; it is obviously over his or her head.

8. A student misses a test or quiz due to an unexcused absence. The student should:
   a. be allowed to take the test the following day, during class time.
   b. be allowed to make up the test during a study hall or a lunch period, or after school.
   c. be allowed to take a different, slightly more difficult version of the test.
   d. be given a zero. Taking the same test would give the student an advantage, since other students will have discussed the test. Creating a new test would take too much time.

Essay section: Your essay should be at least one full page and must be double-spaced. Use scrap paper to collect your thoughts and develop an outline (hint, hint), but use a clean piece of paper for the final draft. Write in complete sentences, using proper punctuation, and remember—neatness counts.

Discuss whether a student who does not complete homework assignments but who earns the highest grades on tests should be penalized for the incomplete assignments. Be sure to discuss whether zeros should be calculated for every incomplete assignment, as well as how heavily homework should weigh in the final grade. If you argue that the student should not be penalized with zeros, describe at least two creative alternatives.

ANSWER KEY AND EXPLANATIONS
True/False

1. False. Since one reason schools grade is to sort and rank their students, many teachers feel compelled to give grades that accomplish this task. While a few teachers might want to award everyone in class an A if everyone did fabulous work, studies reveal most teachers do not. Besides, no teacher wants to be known as a "softy" or for teaching a "gut" course.

2. False. Clearly some teachers are more lenient than others. Even in math, which is regarded as the easiest and least controversial subject to grade, evidence shows that grading is highly subjective. In one study, 138 teachers were asked to grade a student's geometry test. The result was a remarkable range of grades, from a 28 (a low F) to a 95 (an A).[2] Furthermore, when teachers grade on a curve (see Chapter 6), the grades vary depending on the performance of classmates and on the teacher's system of grade distribution. For instance, in a class of 30 students, a more lenient teacher might distribute grades this way: 9 A's, 9 B's, 10 C's, 2 D's and no F's. A more demanding teacher might distribute only 2 A's, 6 B's, 13 C's (after all, isn't C supposed to be average?), 5 D's, and 4 F's.

3. True. If the majority of the class fails a test, some teachers throw out the test and go over the material again, reasoning that either they didn't teach the material adequately or the test did not cover the material taught. Other teachers adjust their grading scale so that the majority of the students earn a B or C grade, depending on which the teacher considers average. While this may work to your advantage, as when an F becomes a C, it has pitfalls as well. E. Ray Dockery, an associate professor of education at Winthrop University in South Carolina, recalls a time when one of his college professors announced that a 93 was the minimum grade for an A. At the end of the semester, when the professor realized that many students had averages of at least a 93, he raised the cut-off for an A to 94. Dockery's average was 93.5, and he still remembers his disappointment at not getting the A he thought he deserved.[3]

4. True. While some educators view an F as a spur to work harder, most see it as a sign of failure. Does an F mean you did not learn anything? Perhaps, but not always. In a challenging class it may take a student longer to absorb the information. He or she may finish the course with the same mastery as an A or B student, but may have mastered the material after the test (or the deadline). The grade is not representative of the overall picture, but it is still an F on the report card.

Multiple-Choice

Questions 5–8 are hypothetical situations that many teachers encounter. Answers for these questions will vary, depending on your (and your teacher's) personal opinion. But your opinion is valued here, unlike on some tests.

In general, teachers either emphasize grades or find them a nuisance.[4] The teachers who care about grades, and about sorting and ranking their students, tend to say, "The paper cannot be done over; you had your chance!" or "A test cannot be retaken to improve a low grade" or "Work cannot be made up from unexcused absences such as suspensions and cutting class." In these classes, even if you have mastered the material, your grade will be low if you don't hand in all homework and projects on time. Also, grade-oriented teachers tend to grade everything, including nonacademic factors such as neatness, correct form (did you follow the instructions *exactly?*), and presentation.

In contrast, teachers who teach for learning and care less about grades tend to say, "You may continue to revise your paper. I hope you will keep working on it until you have earned an acceptable grade." They will let you retake a test or take a new version of a test, and make up missed work. Their goal is to keep you wanting to learn more and do better.

Essay

When students perform well on tests and do not need to reinforce skills and concepts through homework, they may blow off their homework as pencil-pushing busywork, or do the work and chalk it up as an inescapable fact of life. Sometimes students want to do their work but are swamped with personal matters. Whether you think these students should have to do their homework may depend on which type of student you relate to most. Do you question the purpose of your homework? Or do you think it is important, and not that difficult, to play by the rules and do what needs to be done to get a good grade?

Either way, when zeros are calculated into a student's average, the average is skewed. One educator who feels that zeros are unfair states, "One of the most punitive and damaging

Homework can be seen as a chore, or as part of school life.

weapons in a teacher's grading arsenal is the use of zeros."[5] The problem of including zeros when calculating an average is demonstrated in this calculation of an average temperature for one week.[6]

Suppose the temperatures at noon each day were:

Sunday: 92
Monday: 91
Tuesday: 90
Wednesday: 80
Thursday: 84
Friday: 85
Saturday: 82

If we add the temperatures together and divide by 7 to calculate the average, we will get 86. But let's say we forgot to get a reading for Wednesday (the coldest day) and we calculate that day's temperature as zero. If we add the temperatures together and divide by 7 the new average will be 74, even though the temperature was never below 80 on any day.

What alternative methods could you use? The Toronto school district asks teachers to calculate the median grade rather than the average grade. The median is the grade that falls directly in the middle when grades are put into numerical order. To calculate the median you eliminate the highest and the lowest numbers until only one is left, with an equal number of figures above and an equal number below. (With an even number of entries, you average the last two remaining to find the median.) Using the temperature example:

	92	
3 above	91	
	90	
	85	Median
	84	
3 below	82	
	80	

The median temperature is 85 degrees (one degree off the average). If you don't have a reading for Wednesday and assign a zero, the median is 87.

Another approach would be to disregard the Wednesday reading and calculate the average using only the other figures. Adding them and dividing by 6, instead of 7, would give you an average of 87, a fairly reliable reading.

Another solution teachers can use is to not give grades lower than 10 points below the lowest passing grade. So if 60 is the lowest a student can receive on a test and still pass, the teacher would not give a score of less than 50. This would counter the large number of possibilities for an F compared to other grades.[7] Or teachers can report "insufficient information to score, incomplete, or in progress" instead of a zero, which conveys no information.[8] As one parent-teacher noted, "I will be a better partner in my child's education if I know that she is irresponsible rather than conclude that she is failing to learn."[9]

CHAPTER 4

What Turns You On?

Brad is an enthusiastic reader who also loves to write and to create art. He's bright, talented, and interested in mythology, music, and the outdoors. But Brad and math don't click. At first, Brad worked hard to understand the concepts. He even asked a friend in an advanced math class to help him study. But after working hard and still earning D's and F's on his tests, Brad began to see himself as incapable of learning. He gave up trying—first in math, then in all his classes except art.

Even after Brad blew off school, he continued to read a book a night and write about it in his journal. He knew the dates of every Grateful Dead concert, what songs were played, and in what order. And he could tell fabulous stories about every mythological character.

It is not surprising that Brad became frustrated with school. What he was expected to learn did not seem interesting or useful to him. His only motivation was to get a good grade so that his parents would get off his back. However, when Brad worked on projects or read about subjects that fascinated him, he would lose himself in the material, and hours would pass without his realizing it.

INTERNAL VS. EXTERNAL MOTIVATION

If you read for your own enjoyment or because you are curious about a topic (as was Brad with mythology and Grateful Dead concerts), you are internally motivated. If your only reason for reading is that your parents pay you for every book, you are externally motivated. Your reason for reading is the money, not because you enjoy reading or learning. Any time you do something to receive a reward (perhaps money, privileges, or praise) or to avoid a punishment (such as being nagged, or grounded), you are externally, or extrinsically, motivated.

Judging from your own experience, which type of motivation do you think is the strongest? Keep your response in mind as you walk through these four scenarios.

When you study or read because someone says you must, your motivation is external.

Scenario 1: You enter a writing contest in which the prize is a million dollars. Contestants have two hours to write a page of dialogue about anything. On your mark, get set, GO.

Are you feeling pressured? Have you developed your characters yet? What is going through your mind? Are you coming up with ideas, or are you thinking about what you'd do with your prize money? If you've worked out a dialogue, are you pleased with it? The stakes are high, so this writing needs to be the best that you can produce in the time given. It's not easy to let your mind go free, is it?

Scenario 2: Your English teacher asks you to write a page of dialogue about anything you'd like. The assignment is due in a week and will be graded. You haven't done as well as you would have liked in this class, so your goal is to earn at least a B+.

How are you doing? Is it easier, harder, or the same, to write this dialogue as to write the one that could win you a million dollars?

Scenario 3: Picture the same English class, same assignment, except this time the dialogue will not be graded. It's an exercise to free your mind and help you create characters for a short story you will work on later in the semester. Nobody is going to read the dialogue but you. What do you think about the process now?

Scenario 4: This time you are hanging out with a friend. A man with a purple-and-green mohawk walks by. He is wearing spangled leather pants and silver boots, pushing a stroller occupied by a monkey in a lavender bonnet. You and your friend do double-takes and break down laughing. You wonder who this man is and what his life is like. For fun, you and your friend start a dialogue between the man and his parents the first time he brings his monkey home for a visit. Your ideas start flying between bouts of laughter.

Catch our drift? The dialogue probably got a little easier to write in each scenario. The last one practically wrote itself. There, the character was already created, so that took you off the hook a bit. But you were also internally motivated. The man inspired you to create a scene, but you were creating the dialogue because you wanted to. Even though scenario 3, the free-writing assignment, was prompted by a teacher, you could be internally motivated to write it for your own pleasure, since only you would read it. We say "could" because sometimes students are so conditioned to think that every assignment counts that they have a hard time writing for themselves.

Can you see that the first two experiences are different from the last two? Was your original idea of which type of motivation was stronger the same as your last thoughts on the issue? Do you think the first two assignments were more challenging. Or do you think that they were more exciting, and therefore more fun, because a reward was dangled before you?

THE STUDENT'S LIFE

Studies of the role of grading show that students generally care about learning, or care about grades, or care about both learning and grades, or care about neither. Since learning is an internal motivator and grades are an external motivator, the type of student you are affects your experience in school. And although they are only stereotypes, students in each category tends to share similar characteristics and personality traits.[1] Which type of student are you?

The passionate learner:

    gets the Greek scholar award

    is willing to learn material not on the test

    has excellent study skills

    is a confident test taker

    is most likely to think for himself or herself

The give-me-my-diploma-and-let-me-be-a-success-in-life student:

    feels the most pressure to get good grades

    is nervous about tests and large projects

    doesn't question established ideas or practices

    tends to think like the teacher

School populations usually include many types—from passionate learners to those who are turned off by school.

is not overly creative

has poor study skills because he or she doesn't enjoy studying

takes only classes in which he or she expects to do well

The I-want-it-all student:

wants to reap rewards for good grades and learn along the way

relies on grades to know how he or she is doing

tends to be outgoing and friendly

thinks realistically about situations and ideas

is uneasy and panicky during tests

The turned-off student:

is not motivated in school

is easily frustrated

is stressed out by school

is often shy within the school walls

is most likely to drop out of school

THE REALITY OF THE SITUATION

On the surface, rewards and punishments work well, are fun, and effffective. Dogs love treats and people love medals, money, and positive feedback. Nobody enjoys punishments, and most people will work to avoid them. But let's take out the magnifying glass and look more closely at what rewards and punishments do.

Our dog Skipper has been trained to go into the backyard in the evening and "do his business." When he comes back into the house he scratches on the bin where his treats are kept, demanding a reward. Skipper is now older and wiser. He gets his treat and then scratches on the door to be let out again—hoping for another treat.

Our point? Rewards and punishments create a situation where the result (gaining the reward or avoiding the punishment) becomes more important than the task. Also, it is often easy to find a shortcut to the reward. Think about it. Your parents announce that you can't go out with your friends until you have cleaned your room. The only motive you have for cleaning it is to get to go out. Will you take as much time and care cleaning as if you were sick of the clutter and ready to conquer the disaster?

Our bet is that you will rush through the job, doing the minimum. You may turn on the vacuum while you straighten the bed to give the impression that you have gone the distance. And when your friends arrive, you will probably rush off before your parents have a chance to inspect.

It might have gotten the job done, but it certainly wasn't pretty. Furthermore, you probably didn't enjoy the process. By placing the emphasis on the result, rewards and punishments de-emphasize the process or the satisfaction that the process can bring.

Another negative effect is that once rewards have become established, it is difficult to move away from them. Research shows that the more people are rewarded, the more they need a reward.[2] But if rewards and punishments have never been used, they are often not necessary.

If you are used to receiving money for taking out the garbage, chances are you will stop taking out the garbage if you no longer get paid. If your parents add another chore, such as mowing the lawn, you may expect to get paid for the new chore as well. However, if you take out the garbage when

Gaining the reward can become more important than the task.

it is full (because your parents have emphasized the importance of contributing to the family) and your parents then ask you to mow the lawn, it would probably not occur to you to expect money.

On a slightly different note, rewarding a person for something he or she likes doing can devalue the activity and send a negative message: "Here, I'll give you this incentive because I think this task is not worth doing for its own sake." An example of this confusing message is a pizza chain's program called "Book It," which rewards children with free pizza certificates for reading books. Offering a pizza reward sends a message that "reading is not worthwhile on its own, so we'll give you a reason to read." The message is even more confusing because the reward is unrelated to the activity. Why pizza? Why not reward reading with more books?[3]

A CONFLICT OF INTEREST

When grades are used as incentives for learning, and not just as tools for evaluating performance, they serve as a system of rewards and punishments. And, as we've seen, using rewards and punishments is often not a good idea. In school, externally motivating students encourages them to do only what they need to do to get an acceptable grade, and nothing more. It encourages students to cram for tests, which means they forget the material after the test is over. Emphasis on grades may lead to increased cheating,[4] may encourage students to adopt views that match those of the teacher, and may lead to a loss of interest in learning. Low grades prompt students to think of themselves as dumb, even if they are able students, and may lead some students to drop out of school.

Now think about an additional negative effect of grades. In learning complex material, or information based on reasoning, individuals often go through a process of confusion before they can make sense of the material. When every assignment is graded, students can't experiment with different thoughts and processes.

So what's the answer—to eliminate grades? So many students rely on grades as their primary reason for working in school that it would be difficult to simply drop grades. We'd need to restructure school as we know it today. Students would need to learn the value of studying. Many teachers wouldn't know how to teach without the power of grades to keep order and control in the classroom. Dangling a grade before you or threatening you with a bad grade is easy and, more times than not, effective.

Sometimes students are asked to learn something that does not seem important or useful. If the material doesn't interest them, what reason other than grades would they have for learning it? This is when grades can be handy; they can create the necessary challenge when the task is to study something that seems meaningless and irrelevant.

Ideally, students would understand that learning does for

your mind what pushups or weight lifting does for your muscles—it builds strength and endurance. Learning is largely about accumulating knowledge, sorting through the knowledge, and eventually making sense of the knowledge. The purpose of studying should not be to memorize facts for a test so that you can earn a good grade and please your parents. Ideally, studying should teach you how to become a lifetime learner. But it is obvious that using grades to motivate is often easier and quicker. Educators rationalize that some motivation is better than none, and to an extent, they are right. But external motivation should be a last resort, not a standard practice.

HOW ARE YOU SMART (NOT *ARE* YOU SMART)?

Who is smarter—an articulate, well-read student with an impressive vocabulary, or someone who can rebuild a broken-down car and make it run smoothly? The literary student probably has a higher GPA than the car mechanic, but Howard Gardner, who developed the theory of multiple intelligences, challenges the traditional notion that one is any "smarter" than the other. They are both intelligent, he explains, just in different ways. If your car breaks down on the highway, who would you like to see pull up to help, "a professor with a Ph.D. or a car mechanic with a junior high education?"[5] Today, the professor probably has a car phone you could use to call AAA, but you will eventually rely on the mechanic.

Gardner, a neuroscientist who formerly worked with brain-injured patients, is now a professor of cognition and education at Harvard Graduate School of Education. He believes that schools place too much emphasis on linguistic intelligence (word smart) and logical/mathematical intelli-gence, and give too little value to spatial intelligence (visual or picture smart), body-kinesthetic intelligence, musical in-telligence, interpersonal intelligence (people smart), or in-trapersonal intelligence (being in tune with oneself).[6] In recent years, Gardner has added another intelligence to his list, naturalist intelligence (nature smart), and is debating whether to add a ninth, existentialist intelligence.[7]

Gardner is not the first person to report various types of intelligences. What makes Gardner's theory unique, is that it is scientifically based.[8] Before a skill, talent, or ability is given the title "intelligence," Gardner ensures that it meets his four criteria.

1. Each intelligence has its own expressive language or system of symbols (linguistic intelligence has words, musical intelligence has different notes or tones, body-kinesthetic has movements, facial expressions and gestures).

2. Each intelligence must be biologically based and rooted in a specific location in the brain, which can be identified. As an example, after a stroke, a person may be unable to speak but able to harmonize to music. This is because linguistic intelligence is based pri-marily in the left hemisphere of the brain while musi-cal, spatial, and interpersonal intelligence are based in the right hemisphere.

3. Each intelligence must be able to grow and develop throughout a person's lifetime.

4. Each intelligence must be culturally valued in society.

If you don't do well in school, your strength may be in one of the intelligences not emphasized in the traditional class-

Howard Gardner's theory of multiple intelligences suggests that people can be "smart" in different ways. Here a student displays spatial intelligence while applying architectural principles to the design of a pumpkin.

room. The theory of multiple intelligences may explain some of the frustration you feel. But, although MI theory can offer insight into your situation, it doesn't give you permission to ignore your weaknesses, or to totally blow off school. (Nice try though!) Gardner emphasizes that students should work on all of their intelligences, especially those that are weaker. Knowing that you have strengths in areas not as appreciated in the classroom can help you gain a healthier perspective on your grades and a more positive attitude toward school.

CHAPTER 5
Doing It Differently: Schools That Do Not Grade

Get a hold of this—some schools give no grades, use no tests, and set no deadlines. In fact, in some schools, classes are optional. That's right, at democratic schools, also known as free schools, classes are not mandatory. Children as young as four have as much freedom and responsibility as the adults in the community. Classes are offered, but the students are never told or even encouraged to attend. Students can choose not to go to any classes for a year and no one will challenge them—as long as they are not disruptive to others.

A. S. Neill founded the British school, Summerhill, in 1921. It is one of the oldest free schools still operating. Neill's main concern was not academic learning. His view was that children learn what they want to learn, no matter how it is taught, and disregard what they don't think is important, useful, or interesting. He recognized that book learning has a role, but he believed that personality and character (who you

48

are) are equally important. Neill's goal was to help students find happiness because he thought that personal happiness was central to a good life. With happiness, he believed, all else falls into place.

Recently, the British government announced that it would shut down Summerhill unless changes were made to ensure that the school's students were not just goofing off all day. The government was not suggesting that the school institute grading, since schools in England do not use grades to assess students. (To enter college or university, students take a General Certificate of Secondary Education exam in the subjects they wish to study.) The government wanted the Summerhill staff to evaluate students' performance and track their academic achievements and progress.

The idea that students are capable of self-motivated learning is challenging for some people. Even educators at Summerhill, and schools like it around the world, admit that their "child-centered approach" is not for everyone. For students used to traditional schools, the free-school environment can produce culture shock, and some students have a difficult time adjusting to the freedom. Neill observed that it typically took these students a year before they were ready to attend classes on their own and take charge of their own learning. Some students, he wrote, never adjusted and these, he believed, should return to more structured schools.

To save the school, Summerhill took the British government to court. The students, staff, and employees of the school piled into the Royal Courts of Justice in London for the trial. In the end, the justices decided that "learning is not confined to lessons and acknowledge[d] the right of children not to attend them."[1] They also said that the voices of the children should be heard the next time the school was inspected by government officials.

If government officials visited your school, what would you tell them? Could you outline what you were learning? And would you be as determined to save your school? Now envision your ideal school. We can't read your minds, but it is our hunch that a school like the one you envision exists somewhere in the world. There are almost 7,000 alternative and independent schools in the United States. Think how many there must be around the world.[2] And they are all different.

WHAT REPLACES GRADES?

While some alternative schools use grades, many do not. What methods do they use to assess student learning?

Credit/No Credit. At Independent High School, a non-graded public high school in Richmond, Virginia, each course is assigned a certain number of credits. Students earn full credit, partial credit, or no credit depending on how well they do. Once a student earns a certain number of credits, he or she may graduate.

Is credit/no credit different from a grading system? According to a former Independent High School student, there is more room to negotiate your standing. Teachers require self-evaluations from each student before they make final assessments. The teachers give students feedback throughout the semester but do not make formal evaluations until the class has ended. This gives students time to grow without the pressure of having every move count.

Pass/Fail. A similar system to credit/no credit is pass/fail. Pass represents grades A through D; fail represents F. Pass/fail

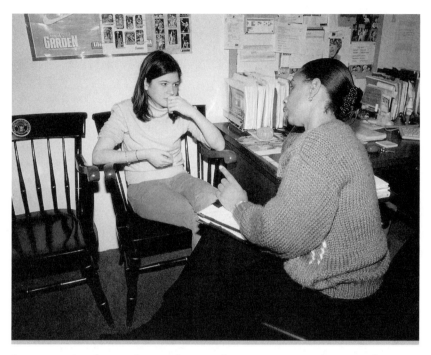

In some schools, teacher-student conferences are used as a technique for assessing student progress.

removes some of the pressure of grades, but not quite as much as with a credit/no credit system. With an F, the student is still penalized for taking the course and failing it. With no credit, the course simply does not appear on the student's records, as if the course had not been taken.

Sometimes colleges that grade will offer courses outside a student's concentration as pass/fail. This encourages students to take classes they might avoid for fear of a low grade that would blot their academic record.

Interestingly, some students who take courses on a pass/fail basis earn the equivalent of an A in the course. One professor believes that excelling is simply in some people's nature. She thinks that students who care enough about their grades to go through the paperwork required to take a course pass/fail are also the ones who automatically put forth the effort needed to succeed. (This professor may not appreciate how motivated slackers can be to slack!)

A college student offered a different reason for her A-caliber work in a pass/fail class. She noted that pass/fail removed the pressure and allowed her to focus all her attention on the material rather than the grade.

Written evaluations. Written evaluations are more descriptive than pass/fail, credit/no credit, or grades. Instead of summarizing a student's performance by a letter or number, teachers provide feedback in narrative form. Evaluations are based on a student's strengths and weaknesses. Teachers may occasionally give a test, but exams are not routine. Instead, students are expected to complete papers that demonstrate an understanding of the topic or an active effort toward grasping the issues.

How do science and math classes work if there are no tests? Classes are directed more toward application than memorization. Instead of being tested on formulas needed to complete a calculation, students are asked to conduct an experiment in which calculations are needed.

Portfolios. Portfolios are often used in the art world, to show the range of an artist's work. They are used in selecting artists for an exhibit, and also for job or college or graduate school applications. Many schools that do not grade find portfolios a helpful technique, and encourage students to create work portfolios. These may include papers, self-evaluations, teacher evaluations, projects, pictures, videos, and other work samples.

A high school student (left) presents her course portfolio to a review board.

WHEN THE CHOICE IS YOURS—UNGRADED COLLEGES

You may not have the option of choosing your middle school or your high school. That may depend on your parents and where you live. But if ungraded schools appeal to you, you may want to consider a college that does not grade. Some are Hampshire College in Amherst, Massachusetts; Evergreen College in Olympia, Washington; Warren Wilson College outside Asheville, North Carolina; Bennington College in Bennington, Vermont. Brown University in Providence, Rhode Island, has an ungraded option.

However, don't imagine that ungraded schools are easier than graded schools. With a grade, you typically stop with an

A. With no grade, you have no way to know how well you are doing compared with other students. This ambiguity drives some students crazy. Or it may encourage them to push themselves past their ordinary comfort zones, to reach a place where breakthroughs and creativity flourish.

As educators acknowledge, not every school is suitable for every student. While alternative schools may be ideal for some, they require self-motivation, discipline, and initiative. So know who you are! If you are a grade-lover who needs grades to study, why choose a school that doesn't grade? If you do not enjoy working for grades and would rather learn at your own pace, exploring tangents as they appear, an ungraded school might be the place for you.

As Hampshire College's motto states, "To Know Is Not Enough." There is an infinite amount of knowledge to be learned in the world. It is impossible to know it all. Thus the question is: Is the purpose of school to teach information or to give students the skills to learn throughout a lifetime? A Yiddish proverb (in a way) offers a response: "To every answer you can find a new question." The more educated you become, the more you will discover how much you still do not know.

CHAPTER 6

Knowing Where You Stand

I'm Nobody! Who are you?
Are you—Nobody—too?

These lines were written by Emily Dickinson, a reclusive poet who left a trove of now-treasured poems when she died. As the poem suggests, Dickinson had no idea she would one day be ranked among America's best-loved poets.

Unlike Emily Dickinson, you probably know your status in school. This awareness will stay with you all your life. Unless you are one of the rare birds who is home-schooled, de-schooled, or attending an ungraded school, you know whether you are an A, B, C, or D student. Indeed most students, according to Alfie Kohn, author of *No Contest: The Case Against Competition*, are so addicted to grades that their absence creates an "existential vertigo"—*Who am I, if not a B+?*[1]

Eventually, too, you will know your grade point average,

or GPA, that precise decimal-point average of your letter grades. And if that isn't enough to let you know your status on the totem pole, sometime in your senior year you will be informed of your class rank—how you place amid all your classmates. This rank may be as simple as top (or bottom) half of your class or as exact as number 257 out of 350 students. School districts get ranked, too. A list of the top 100 school districts appears annually. And Leon Botstein, president of Bard College, gave the entire system a grade of F because of its failure to keep most high school students interested in real learning, or to treat them as adults.[2]

From the earliest school years, students are made aware of how well or poorly they are doing in comparison to their classmates.

Ranking is an all-American obsession. Each year, *U.S. News and World Report* assigns every U.S. college and university a rank. Amazon.com, the online bookseller, designates a sales rank for each book it sells (imagine what it feels like to be 647,246 on that list). We grade our restaurants, neighborhoods, and eggs and butter. *People* magazine compiles an annual list of the 50 most beautiful people, while *Fortune* names the wealthiest. Another poll tells us if our president is on or off the most admired list.

Historically, and in some societies still, your status in life, your rewards, and your opportunities, depend not on your talent, hard work, or even luck. Instead, they depend on your family's status in society, and perhaps on your gender. Thus, if you are a male and born into a rich, aristocratic family, you will be *entitled* to a good education, regardless of your effort, talent, or intelligence. If you are instead born into poverty, you will surely be denied such an opportunity. (This system is called an aristocracy, and our Constitution is a direct revolt against it.)

In contrast, when hard work, talent, or extraordinary intelligence can pave a road to success—as when a poor immigrant's daughter earns a scholarship to an Ivy League school—the system of rewards and opportunities is called a meritocracy. In education, the idea of meritocracy took an interesting turn when educators at Harvard in the 1940s decided to create an elite student body. Instead of accepting only the sons of wealthy Harvard alumni and graduates of exclusive New England boarding schools, the administrators decided to base admissions on merit. Poor but bright students were recruited from other areas and were awarded scholarships and the chance to gain a fine education. Harvard expected to create an elite corps of individuals—elite for their education, not their birthright. With access to a fine education, and then to the best jobs, the brightest and the best would become the guardians of our nation—"philosopher kings" who would lead us to greatness.[3] According to Nicholas Lemann, author of *The Big Test*, a history of meritocracy, the educated elite don't always reach this lofty goal. However, the rewarding of excellence plays a significant role in education, especially in the selection of students at schools

In a merit-based system, hard work and ability are rewarded. These students earned scholarship awards in a national science talent search.

noted for high standards. Today, a belief in meritocracy explains why those who demonstrate ability are rewarded with honors, advantages, and perks—including the honor roll, advanced placement and honors classes, Merit Scholarships, and admission to selective schools. In short, it is why we continue to rank and sort, in school and everywhere else.

SO WHAT'S THE PROBLEM?

Clearly, competition, grading, ranking, and sorting are firmly rooted in our society. Yet two centuries after competition and ranking based on grades began, some outspoken critics argue that the practice of ranking and sorting students cannot be justified, and does not work especially well in the classroom. These are some of their major concerns:

Ranking labels people unfairly and unnecessarily. As critic John Gatto says in his book, *Dumbing Us Down*, with grades and rank "you come to know your place"—a place, he suggests, that may not be accurate or very important in the larger picture of life. Another critic, Alfie Kohn, suggests, "you come to believe that your self worth as a person is somehow connected to your grade and your rank."[4] Poor students begin to think they are bad people.

You would think that good students would feel good about their good grades, but they, too, can be misled by grades and ranking. Instead of perceiving a B as good, ambitious students might see it as a "failure to get an A," and thus see themselves as failures. We know, too, that a series of failures breeds a sense of defeat. Two-thirds of students who drop out of school had been consistently receiving bad grades.[5]

Ranking is inaccurate and unreliable. According to Ohmer Milton, Howard Pollio, and James Eison, authors of *Making Sense of College Grades*, a GPA doesn't really say enough about a student to be of much value. While grades may accurately measure a person's verbal and math skills, they are poor measures of other "intelligences," such as ability to get along with people and creativity, which are essential to success. In one study of engineers, those who had lower GPA's but could get along with people achieved greater job success than did engineers with better grades and higher GPA's.

Another problem, says Pollio and his colleagues, is that class rank is an inadequate way to compare students. The GPA of a student who earned A's in science and math but D's in everything else can be the same as a student who earned all C's. Looking at their GPA's, which one will you trust to design a bridge?

We also know that students who get good grades (and especially those whose parents care the most about their grades) do two things that skew the validity of a GPA. First, they tend to drop or avoid courses in which they feel they won't get a good grade. More courageous students, and those who care about learning more than about grades, may have lower GPA's, when, in fact, they are better students. Further, we know that students who really care about learning are less likely to cheat.[6]

The point is, if grades (and therefore GPA and class rank) are sometimes unreliable predictors of future success, and so relative, why give them so much power? Consider this scenario (and downside to GPA's). Joe may have a 3.50 GPA and get into law school. You may have a 3.49—only 100th of a decimal point lower—and be rejected.[7] And that 100th of a point difference was because you handed in your well-written term paper a few days late. One-hundredth of a GPA point is a small difference; but in a situation such as this, it becomes huge, and obviously more significant than it deserves to be.

GPA is a meaningless number. According to Pollio, Milton, and Eison, we assign too much value to a GPA when we work it out to more decimal places than were in the original numbers we are averaging.[8] Going from a simple 5-point (A, B, C, D, F) system, to a 400-point decimal system (4.00, 3.99, 3.98, 3.97, and we are only at 4 of the 400 possibilities!), makes the GPA *appear* to be complex and highly accurate. Alas, in reality, it is quite imprecise and therefore meaningless.

WE CAN'T HAVE IT BOTH WAYS

Research and common wisdom suggest that we cannot have it both ways: We cannot use grades to promote learning and teaching at the same time that we use grades to rank and sort students. The two goals are incompatible.

Ranking requires different kinds of tests—tests that yield

objective measurements (in order to be "fair"). These could be multiple-choice, fill-in-the-blank, true or false, and matching tests. Yet we know that essay exams are better ways to allow students to show what they have learned in problem solving, or how well they understand a subject. Ranking also produces different kinds of students—those who are more inclined to cheat, who care more about what will be on the test than about learning for the sake of learning, who avoid courses in which their grade might threaten their rank.

A little competition, especially when it is voluntary and playful as in sports and games, is fun. And many people believe schools should foster competitiveness to prepare students for the "real world." But competition in school cannot be compared to competition in the business world, argues John Gatto, one of grading's most outspoken critics. "Competition for grades gives rise to envy and dissatisfaction."[9]

Competition has many drawbacks. The first, and most basic, is that each competitor is essentially trying to outdo the

Competition in sports and games can be fun, and adds a challenge. Competition for grades can be harmful.

next person. It is also easy to get carried away by competition and neglect what is important. In fact, argues Alfie Kohn, competing means that one is working toward a goal in such a way as to prevent others from reaching *their* goals.[10]

Ranking and sorting work against cooperation, by pitting one student against another, with students being the big losers. Trying to be the best can make someone study harder. But studying *harder* is not necessarily the same as studying more *effectively*. In fact, studies have shown that cooperative learning—working with others—is an excellent way to learn and may indeed be better than studying alone.[11]

We live in a competitive society. We are taught to strive for excellence and that excellence is often measured by being on top, being the best. We are taught to believe that competition is in our genetic makeup; that it is human nature; that winning, as Vince Lombardi, the famous football coach, exclaimed, "is the only thing."

Before accepting that competition is natural, consider how much our survival depends on cooperation, on getting along with others, and on depending on them. And think about how much easier and less stressful it is to learn without trying to outdo the next person.

Even if competition is natural, it is not necessarily good. Aggression may be natural too, but that does not mean it is good. Morality means learning to control and limit behaviors that may be natural but are harmful to others or ourselves.

GRADING ON THE CURVE

In 1908 Professor Max Meyer of the University of Missouri failed every student in his class. When the administration protested his action, Meyer surveyed his colleagues' grading practices. What he found surprised him: Every professor had a different standard for assigning grades.

At the time, interest was growing in the study of intelligence. One prevailing theory held that intelligence is unevenly distributed through the population; a few people are very smart, most people are average, and a few are below average. Working from this theory, Meyer decided that if intelligence and grades go hand in hand (which they may not, but he never read this book), there should be only a few A's, many average grades, and a few below-average grades in a class. This distribution of grades follows what is called a bell-shaped curve (see illustration to understand why).

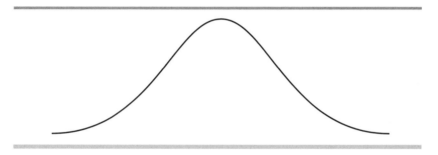

Professor Meyer now adjusted his distribution of grades to follow this theory. For a class of 30 students he determined that the top 3 percent would get A's, the next 22 percent would receive B's, the middle 50 percent would get C's, the next 22 percent would get D's, and the bottom 3 percent would fail (receive F's).

Why Meyer determined that the top 3 percent were superior—and not the top 1 percent, or 10 percent—remains a mystery. Yet many teachers began to use the grade curve, perhaps because Meyer had described his theory in the prestigious journal, *Science*. If it was in *Science*, assumed thousands of teachers and school administrators, then it must be correct.

Grading on a curve is much less prevalent today, but some teachers still grade this way. They hand out mostly average grades, no matter who is in the class, what they learned or failed to learn, or what the teacher taught or failed to teach. Thus in a science class full of geniuses, perhaps at the Bronx High School of Science or M.I.T., only one or two students in a class of thirty will receive an A. Another one or two are destined to fail. Sure, many teachers now skew the curve upward and are more liberal about giving A's and B's and more reluctant to flunk students who really try. Yet few teachers are willing to flunk an entire class for not learning enough, or to give A's to an entire class that has mastered the material.

Besides handing out inaccurate assessments, grading on the curve pits one student against another, to vie for the few A's and B's and avoid the inevitable D's and F's. Indeed, grading on the curve probably represents grading and competition at their worst.

WHEN THE ODDS ARE IN YOUR FAVOR

Grade inflation—where students get higher marks than they deserve—presents a totally different problem. (Getting an inflated grade is a bit like finding a ten-dollar bill on the ground at the ballpark. Are you *really* going to try to find out who lost it?) If grades are supposed to provide feedback about what you have learned, then an inflated grade, while getting your parents off your back and looking great on your school record, gives you a false sense of accomplishment. It's like looking into a mirror—in a fun house.

Teachers of social sciences and English tend to be more

64

Grade Inflation

Percent of college freshman who said their high school grade average was:

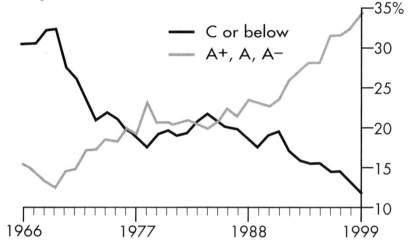

UCLA Higher Education Research Institute

liberal in awarding high grades. "Hard science" teachers, in math and chemistry, tend to be more parsimonious, awarding fewer high marks.

In 1999 the economy of the United States was thriving. So, it seemed, were grades and students' feelings about them. Grade inflation was at a peak (see chart). But no one seemed to care, since students reported feeling great about their school performance.[12] In an annual survey conducted by UCLA, nearly 60 percent of students rated their scholastic abilities as above average or in the top 10 percent.[13]

Given how deeply entrenched competition is in our society, we recognize it would be difficult to abandon it altogether. When competition is voluntary and when you can maintain a healthy perspective, who are we to argue against the joy of outsmarting your smug neighbor in math class? So be competitive if you will. Just don't start crying about your grades or boasting about your class rank, because it doesn't mean much in the whole picture of life (unless you hope to be an orthopedic surgeon). Best to remember the wisdom of Popeye, "I am what I am I am." That ought to be good enough.

CHAPTER 7

In All Honesty: Does Grading Increase Cheating?

cheat, *v.t.* 1. to take an examination or test in a dishonest way, as by improper access to answers. 2. to violate rules or regulations.

Bob Corbett cheated his way through middle school, cheated his way through high school, and cheated his way through college. Having perfected the art of cheating, he then wrote *The Cheater's Handbook: The Naughty Student's Bible,* an honest, hilarious book about cheating.[1] The blame for cheating, Corbett argues, should be placed on the pressure to get high grades, and on lackluster teaching. "Very rarely does a great teacher have a room full of cheaters," he states. "Make no mistake, though," he warns, "cheating cheats you out of learning, and while not as demanding as real studying, requires a lot of time and preparation."

According to just about every survey on students and cheating, Corbett is giving advice to a large number of willing listeners. In a survey of student leaders listed in *Who's Who Among American High School Students*,[2] 80 percent admitted to cheating at least once.[3] Another study found that 1 in 8 students cheats on an exam in any given class.[4] Nor do students always think that they are doing something wrong or something *that* wrong. Half the students in the *Who's Who* group failed to see cheating as wrong, and nearly all the students (95 percent) who admitted to cheating never got caught.[5]

Among college students fifty years ago, only about 20 percent admitted to cheating. In recent studies, between 75 and 98 percent admit to cheating.[6] Perhaps today's cheaters are

A high percentage of students admit to cheating on exams.

more candid than their grandparents. Nonetheless, cheating appears to be rampant.

With the Internet, electronic devices, and books like *The Cheater's Handbook*, cheating is relatively easy. The inclination to cheat for good grades or simply to pass required courses is often strong. "I'm just trying to do everything I can to get through school," said one student-cheater. "If this is the only way to do it, so be it."[7]

No matter how cheating is rationalized, it is wrong, as Corbett states. Cheating deprives you of the real joy of learning. And you are missing the opportunity to create a foundation for future learning. You also are not giving yourself a chance to find out what you do know. Moreover, even cheaters ought to have consciences and set limits. Corbett suggests, "I don't think it's 'cool' to cheat and go out of your way to do it, when you'd do perfectly fine on your own." He emphasizes that he has paid a personal price for cheating. As an example, he says, "I'm at a loss whenever a hot debate about America's history comes up," then adds, "My ignorance drives me crazy."

As Corbett points out, cheating does more than devalue learning; it gives teachers a false idea of what their students are learning. Cheating hurts teachers who are less skilled or less motivated, and also the excellent teachers, the ones who Corbett believes have the chance to make a positive impact on society. (For alternatives to cheating, see Chapters 11 and 12 on improving your grades.)

SIMPLE AS PIE

The burden for stopping cheating falls on teachers. Students not involved with cheating rarely come forward and "squeal."

To catch cheaters or deter them, more teachers, especially those monitoring standardized tests, rely on sophisticated technology. They also use traditional methods such as distributing different tests, and walking up and down the aisles on guard for cheating glances, crib sheets, and hand signals. However, surveillance often fails to deter cheating or get at the root of it. Most cheaters don't get caught.[8] And while some schools mete out harsh penalties for cheating, including suspension from school, others do not. In one high school, first-time cheaters are punished by a zero grade on the exam, with no notification of parents. In the same school, smoking carries a harsher penalty.

Most students cheat for practical reasons such as not finding time to study, hating the subject, or because they think cheating is easier than studying. With a lot at stake—college entry, scholarships, and pleasing parents—and with the common belief that many people do it, cheating is often difficult to resist.

Sometimes a student may cheat for the thrill of getting away with something that is both risky and wrong. For some students, breaking into the school's electronic record to alter a grade is a way of gaining power that they feel they don't have over their lives. Out-

Teachers often have to take on the responsibility of controlling cheating.

witting the "enemy" carries a certain glamour in the American tradition of rugged individualism.

Ironically, and sadly, some cheating comes from teachers. Under pressure to show good results, some teachers cross the line between helping their students prepare for a test and "teaching for the test" in a way that amounts to cheating. One teacher who wanted her students to do well on a state language contest (and who had helped write the exam) drilled her students in the answers. Her students garnered top awards, but might not have scored so well without her style of "coaching."

One teacher put the answer sheet on top of her desk and then left the classroom for extended periods of time. In another reported incident, a tutor at the University of Minnesota admitted writing hundreds of papers for the school's basketball players.

BLURRED LINES

Exactly what constitutes cheating? And why should cheating matter so much, especially if "everyone" is doing it? The answers aren't always clear. For example, cooperative learning has been shown to be one of the best ways to learn a subject or study for an exam. When, however, does cooperation end and cheating begin? Furthermore, if it is okay to work on a project together, why isn't it okay to do homework assignments together, or to help a classmate with a take-home exam? Learning is supposed to be the purpose of school, not grades. Or is it?

In a *U.S. News and World Report* poll of parents, 20 percent said that doing homework for their children is fair.[9] If a parent is a chemist, what is wrong with working on a science

Working together in study groups or on projects produces cooperative learning.

experiment with a child? Indeed, why shouldn't parents be allowed to teach their children without worrying about whether it borders on cheating?

If parents "helping" too much is considered taboo, tutoring falls into a gray area. In some school districts, where the pressure to get into a selective college is great, parents pay tutors $45 an hour or more just to help a child with homework. Tutoring for standardized tests, such as the SAT, commands rates as high as $150 an hour. The top specialists, those who write the books, get $450-$500 an hour. Why isn't this tutoring considered cheating?

If we want to teach self-reliance, then these forms of help—from fellow students, parents, tutors, or even the classic *Cliff Notes*—do constitute cheating. If we are teaching students not to procrastinate and to learn to meet deadlines, then getting out of an exam to have an extra day to study fails to serve them well. On the other hand, if we place less emphasis on grades and more on learning, we might be glad to see students working and learning in ways that we now call cheating or perhaps those gray areas around the edges of cheating.

SOMETHING TO PONDER

If grading encourages cheating, then ungraded schools ought to have less cheating. Chris Sperry teaches at an ungraded school in upstate New York. Most of the students are college-bound, but come from families less anxious about academic competition. "I would like to think that our students are more moral and won't cheat for higher reasons," observes Sperry, "but I wouldn't put my money on that. I think mostly they just have less opportunity and reason to cheat than do their peers in traditional schools.[10]

In schools with no tests, teachers assess their students' work at individual conferences and from watching them demonstrate their knowledge in performances or presentations, creative projects, journal entries, and the like. Work is so individualized that cheating is difficult. Most important, without grades or ranking, students can focus on actual learning instead of worrying about grades.

Abolishing grades eliminates the fear of getting poor ones. This gives students greater incentive and courage to take courses in which they might earn poor grades. Students in conventional schools sometimes avoid difficult courses for fear of weakening their GPAs. Sadly, they might love these courses.

We can see why people *think* they need to cheat, but that doesn't mean we accept their reasons. However, people who don't cheat are not necessarily of stronger moral fiber, as the teacher in the ungraded school suggested. They may be afraid, or have less need to cheat. As the stakes for grades go up and the risks of getting caught remain relatively slim, more students may choose to cheat.

How can we stop cheating? We could remove the pressure for good grades and the stigma of bad grades. As in ungraded schools, we could remove grades altogether. Yet even then, cheating—like crime and other immoral behavior—may not disappear. Some people seek the thrill of testing limits, including moral limits. Even replacing tedious studying and dry lectures with fun and entertainment won't solve this problem. Not all learning can be exciting. Some, such as conjugating verbs or learning scientific formulas, *is* rote and boring. But nothing improves a person's self-esteem more than mastering something difficult—the honest way.

CHAPTER 8
Are Grades Coming Between You and Your Teachers?

Y ou've probably had a teacher like Mr. Smith (and if not, at some point in your high school career, you *will*!). Mr. Smith loves to drone on—and on and on and on—about his favorite poem by his favorite poet. You know you will never need or want that information. (For the sake of this discussion, let's assume that you are right.)

While you don't care about the poet or about the obscure poem that relates spiders to death, Smith warns you that you will need to know certain vocabulary words and how spider webs are metaphors for life's woes in order to get a good grade on the upcoming exam. Finally, Smith ends the spider discussion and shows a videotape about Victorian rhyme schemes.

Does Mr. Smith want to abandon grades? You can make a sure bet that he doesn't. In an article on the degrading effect of grading, Alfie Kohn observed that for teachers like Mr.

Some classes can be a bore; and only the fear of failing keeps students from tuning out completely.

Smith, grades are a way to ensure that students pay attention in class, do the assignments, write the papers, and study for the exams. According to Kohn, teachers like Smith moan that "these kids would blow off my course in a minute if they weren't getting a grade for it!"[1] What these teachers are really saying, according to Kohn, is that "without bribes (A's) and threats (F's), students would have no reason to work in the classroom."

In 1945, Dorothy De Zouche, a Missouri teacher, saw through the shallowness of this teaching approach. "If I can't give a child a better reason for studying than a grade on a report card, I ought to lock my desk and go back home and stay there."[2] As De Zouche suggested, grades let too many teachers like Smith off the hook. "Who would be more reluctant to give up grades," asks Kohn, "than a teacher who spends the period slapping transparencies on the overhead projector and lecturing endlessly at students about Romantic poets or genetic codes?"

Good teaching does not require grades, as the history of education proves. The best teachers can convince you that the poet you thought was irrelevant is a wonder, whose poetry grabs your soul. In fact, according to Kohn, study after study shows that students from elementary school to college, all over the world, show *less* interest in learning when they are graded. Nor do most teachers get high marks when the tables are turned and they are graded. In 1999 a Gallup Poll survey asked teenagers to grade their teachers with an A, B, C, D, or F.[3] Only 20 percent gave their teachers an A.

Besides taking teachers off the hook for poor teaching, grades stand between good teachers and their students. Students who are friendly with a teacher are often accused of playing up to the teacher to get a better grade. In turn, teachers who try to mentor individual students are accused of favoritism. As one teacher commented, "I'm tired of being suspicious when students give me compliments, wondering whether they are just trying to get a better grade."[4]

It is difficult for students to trust their teachers to help them when they know the teacher is responsible for judging their work. "Why must I be a teacher and a grader at the same time?" lamented one teacher. "It's like being a parent and an executioner. Or a prosecutor and a judge."[5] On the other hand, some students are motivated to work hard to please a beloved teacher (which is not all bad).

Teacher-and-student relationships can complicate the grades situation. A teacher who dislikes a particular student may try to be fair, but may still grade too harshly. Or, liking a student, a teacher may grade too easily.

Critics of grading argue that when grades are looked at outside the classroom—as when students apply for college, jobs, or scholarships—the teachers gain too much power over the students' lives and futures. If grades were kept in the classroom and used solely to tell teachers and students what is being learned (or still needs to be mastered), then teachers would have less of this kind of power. As an extreme example, during the Vietnam War, when students were not drafted into military service, flunking a college student could mean the difference between his staying in school or his being drafted and perhaps killed or wounded in Vietnam. Many teachers were upset over this power, and some graded leniently, refusing to flunk anyone.

With volunteer armed forces, teachers are no longer burdened with that kind of power. Nevertheless, their grading can make a big difference in a student's life. A teacher's D+ (instead of C-) can mean a student is grounded or suspended from a sports team. A grade of B+ (instead of A-) may keep someone out of a special honors class or from eligibility for certain scholarships.

Besides straining relationships between teachers and students, grading also shapes the way a teacher actually teaches, and how school administrators determine what should be taught. A curriculum oriented toward grading, and especially toward standardized testing, tends to follow what Kohn refers to as a "bunch of facts" approach. Students and teachers more concerned about grades prefer short-answer, true-or-false, and multiple-choice tests over essay exams. They also prefer to teach or study what is going to be assessed, and are

A good relationship between a teacher and students can be strained by the teacher's responsibility for grading the students.

unlikely to explore other areas or delve more deeply or creatively than is required for a good grade. Think about it: if you go out on a limb with an idea, you risk getting it "wrong" on an exam. This risk can cost you a good grade (although you might learn something).

ALL THAT TIME

The average teacher spends many hours each week on grading homework, papers, exams, and other assignments. Would abolishing grades give teachers more time to enrich their own understanding of the subject? A social studies teacher who didn't have to grade could use that time to read newspapers and journals, keep abreast of books in the field, and take courses. However, the claim that grading takes up too much of a teacher's time is somewhat misleading. Without grades, teachers would need some other way of assessing their students' mastery and their own teaching. Alternative methods of assessment—portfolios, conferences, and the like—also take time, often more time than grading. Nor would all teachers use the time saved from grading to improve their teaching or benefit their students.

One argument in favor of grades, and especially standardized test scores, is that they hold mediocre teachers accountable. Grades and test scores are supposed to "prove" not only what a student has learned or failed to learn, but also what a teacher has succeeded in teaching—or failed to teach. However, teachers can be judged without grades, such as by having supervisors observe their classrooms.

UPHOLDING THE TRADITION

Pressure to grade comes from many sources—including teachers. One reason for this may be that people who become teachers and spend their careers in school cared about getting good grades when *they* were students.[6] It is hard to visualize the slacker who always glances at your test papers and blows off homework assignments *wanting* to become a teacher rather than a sports promoter or a web-page designer. Furthermore, a person who cares about learning but not about grades might be drawn to teaching, but might dread working for institutions that insist on grades.

It may be difficult for teachers to give up grading because they are so accustomed to grades. We tend to do what we are taught, observes Carol Sager, teacher and author of *Eliminating Grades in Schools*.[7] Still, according to Alfie Kohn, "Classroom teachers should do everything within their power to make grades as invisible as possible for as long as possible."[8] That may require teaching skills beyond those of the droning Mr. Smith. It may also require greater trust between teachers and students.

Howard Pollio and his colleagues, who have conducted many studies of grading and teaching, offer a possible solution to the teacher-student grade dilemma. They believe that an ideal school would match students who like working for grades with teachers who like teaching for grades. Students who don't care about their grades but care about learning would be matched with teachers who aren't too concerned about grades either.

Abolishing grades is unlikely to occur. Getting rid of all boring teachers is just as unlikely. The challenge, then, is to create schools that foster a *partnership* between teachers and students, one that reflects a more even balance of power than grades currently allow. We can do this only by understanding the role grades play in that partnership—and by not allowing grades to cover up poor teaching or to get in the way of great teaching.

CHAPTER 9

Reaping the Rewards

Although we have been saying that grades aren't everything, remember they are *something*. We want to help you gain a healthy perspective on grades, but we also want to be fair. Getting good grades leads to advantages in our imperfect world. If you can, why not reap some of those rewards? (Just don't get carried away by them.)

More often than not, you get to reap the rewards of your labor. Getting a good grade in a subject that is tough or from a teacher who is a hard grader gives you a feeling of pride and a sense of accomplishment. Since honors or advanced placement classes usually require a lot of hard work, getting an A or even a B in these classes feels good.

For some people studying seems easy, or they don't have to study because they are brilliant. Let's be frank, it is hard to be happy for these natural brains, unless you are one, or they have some redeeming qualities, such as great humility, or per-haps are someone you are dating.

So go ahead. Be a little envious of people who get good grades. According to ethicist Joshua Halberstam, author of *Everyday Ethics* and *Acing College* (a book full of great tips for doing well in any school), envy about grades can serve you well. Despite being one of the "seven deadly sins," envy, according to Halberstam, can be a powerful indicator of what you want for yourself—and can provide the incentive to go af-ter it. If you envy a friend who made the honor roll, why not study hard enough to get on it yourself? Or ask that friend to study with you.

THE PAYOFF

This chapter is for anyone secretly envious of students on the honor roll, or for anyone searching for a reason to work harder for good grades. If you aren't getting good grades, it may be that you need to improve your study skills (see Chap-ters 11 and 12). It could also mean that you need to truly un-derstand that *grades count for something* (even if they aren't *everything*). This insight may hit you in a sudden flash, when you realize that you'll need decent grades to get to do what you want to do—such as be a brain surgeon, an astronaut, a lawyer or scientist. So here's a list to ponder, when you need a good reason for studying when you want to be doing some-thing else.

First and foremost, the reward for good grades is that they make you feel good about yourself and your accomplishment. A good grade seems especially sweet after a difficult exam or a challenging course, or from a teacher who hands out few high grades. And when you think you blew an exam and then learn you aced it, euphoria rushes in, along with a healthy dose of self-esteem.

Good grades create great memories. The effect of most grades, even good ones, may be fleeting, like that of eating chocolate. But sometimes, a particular grade—perhaps for a paper you labored over—yields a memory that lingers for years. Such cherished memories can raise your confidence when things aren't going so well.

Good grades earn the respect of others, especially parents, teachers, and administrators. Most parents appreciate good grades and are generous with praise. And certainly, whether or not your parents would flaunt a MY CHILD IS ON THE HONOR ROLL bumper sticker, you will make them happy. Good grades ensure that you won't get grounded or lose privileges, such as late curfews, the use of the car, or your freedom.

Good grades give you one less thing to worry about.

Good grades let you feel good about yourself and your accomplishments—and may also reap privileges and rewards.

84

They are also one less thing for your parents to get on your case about. While some parents aren't pleased unless you bring home all A's, many parents regard B's (perhaps with a sprinkling of A's) as good. And you can make sure that even a C or a D is appreciated in a class where you were drowning. "But Mom, Dad, I was *flunking* algebra. With a D, I can get a summer job instead of going to summer school."

Good grades guarantee that you can stay on a team or other extracurricular activity. In a suburb of Cleveland, Ohio, a cheerleader was kicked off the squad for bad grades.[1] Her parents filed a federal lawsuit against the school district, claiming that grades ought not to be a criterion for an extracurricular activity such as cheerleading. (It probably would have been a lot easier—and cheaper—to just study harder or hire a tutor, instead of suing the school district.) While some schools have a lax policy on grades or offer extra help, such as study tables or tutoring, many schools require that you maintain average grades to be on a team or in a club.

Good grades give you the chance to get merit scholarships, some worth thousands of dollars. This is not a bad deal if you consider what the scholarship is worth compared to the "cost" of studying.

Good grades give you the opportunity to be accepted by the college of your choice. Most schools that require good grades will not accept students with poor grades—unless their parents are donating a new library, or they are top athletes or have some other extraordinary talent. (See Chapter 14 for a healthy perspective on this issue, in case you aren't getting good grades.)

Good grades give you the chance to take honors and advanced placement classes and seminars. While this may not be everyone's idea of a reward, these classes are usually taught by teachers with knowledge and passion about the subject. Since over a third of teachers are asked to teach subjects they never studied in college,[2] having a teacher who knows and cares about a subject has to be an advantage.

Many teachers show a bias toward students who get good grades. They may reward you by letting you skip the next exam or homework assignment, or they may not care if you snooze through the lectures as long as you maintain the A. While this is not a frequent reward, when it occurs it feels like a true gift from the God of Free Time.

Good grades can reduce your car insurance costs from 10 to 25 percent. This is especially true for males between ages 18 and 25. The reason is that the driving record of this cohort is the worst. Insurance companies (working from statistical evidence) claim that an A student is a safer driver and therefore deserves a cut on the rates.

A little math will show you this is a good deal. If your car insurance is $1,000 a year, getting on the honor roll can save you $100 to $250 a year, which adds up to a stack of CDs, movies, or tickets to a concert or ballpark.

Good grades may get you an interesting internship, such as in a newsroom or a hospital, or on a research project; one that may even involve getting out of school. This internship may, in turn, give you a look at a future profession, and an idea of whether continuing to work for good grades is worthwhile. (Drop out of school and you get a slice of *real* life.)

You can get some of these rewards without good grades. Or maybe you don't care about some of these benefits. But nothing on this list will hurt you. And much on it will make your life a lot sweeter.

With good grades, you might get an interesting internship, or a taste of a possible career.

So, there are rewards for good grades and some—such as scholarships—are quite substantial. But it's important to remember that rewards for grades are not the only rewards in life—and that sometimes the best we can do is *strive for* good grades and accept less. As the poet Robert Browning suggested, a person's reach should exceed his or her grasp.

CHAPTER 10

Living in a Pressure Cooker

It is no surprise that grades are one of the biggest concerns of teenagers. Few schooldays pass without an experience with grades—on homework, papers, tests, or assignments. Those who get good grades usually worry about studying; those who don't get good grades usually worry about their parents' reactions.

In a survey, students in eleven nations were asked how their parents react when they bring home poor grades.[1] From Chile to China, most parents react with anger. Many shout, scold, lecture, criticize, and threaten to punish their children. Some parents punish their children for unacceptable school performances. In the United States, students are often grounded. Spanking and even beating remain the option of other parents.

Fortunately, after the initial blowup, most parents calm down. Many then simply encourage their children to try harder, often warning them of future consequences if bad grades continue. Although it seems increasingly common in the United States, getting a tutor is not a universal solution. What is universal is praise for good grades and requests for an explanation of bad ones.[2]

Many parents will ask for teacher-conferences to discuss bad grades. In Russia, parents usually wait until the teacher requests a conference. In the United States, parents often initiate the conference.

According to research conducted by Howard Pollio, Lee Humphreys, and James Eison, reported in *Making Sense of College Grades*, in the United States parents rather than teachers are the most con-

Poor grades can lead to conflict with a disappointed parent.

cerned about grades. The question is, when can you expect parents to chill some on their worrying? Here's the good news: Most parents let up by the time their children are in college. Here's the bad news: Most parents show the greatest concern when their children are in high school.[3]

If you are having a difficult time getting your parents off your case about not-so-good grades, here's some information for your defense. According to a study by Pollio, Humphreys, and Eison,[4] students whose parents react strongly to bad grades tend to get worse grades than students whose parents show less distress. In addition, those students with intensely worried parents are more likely to cheat—no doubt to keep their parents "pacified." These students also tend to drop courses if they think they will do poorly. Thus they avoid upsetting their parents; although this may not be their only reason for dropping courses.[5]

Under pressure to get good grades and wanting to please their parents, students today spend a fair amount of time doing homework, although on the average, not as much as students did in the past. In a recent survey conducted at UCLA,[6] fewer than a third of the students spent more than six hours a week on homework or studying. In 1987, nearly half spent six or more hours a week on their studies.

Although concerned about their grades, students feel pretty good about themselves. In the UCLA survey, more than 60 percent of first-year college students said they thought they had above-average grades, or had abilities in the top 10 percent.[7] And why not? Many more students than in the past are earning A's and B's, due in part to grade inflation—the overly liberal awarding of high grades.

TEST JITTERS

Test jitters are common, and they don't always go away after the test is over. Years and even decades after graduation, many people report an all-too-familiar dream—or nightmare: They are in a classroom, opening up an exam book and drawing a blank; or they go to class and learn they are having a surprise exam; or they can't find the classroom!

With dreams, you get to wake up. Real life doesn't offer

this out for people who freeze at exams, or shake when called on to give a speech, or cringe when called upon—even when they know the answers.

A little anxiety can actually give you extra energy to keep your memory sharp and your thinking clear. Too much anxiety, though, works against you. The following tips can help you control your anxiety so that it won't get in the way of your thinking clearly or doing well.

Tense, then relax muscle groups. If you feel tense in your jaw or stomach, tighten that muscle even further, hold it, then relax it. Clench your fists, tighten your face, straighten your legs, tense your abdomen, then relax.

Try measured breathing. Focus on your breathing and count slowly as you inhale to the count of 4, hold to the count of 12, and exhale to the count of 8.

Imagine you are someplace relaxing, such as the beach or in your bedroom, listening to great music. Take a fantasy trip to someplace that makes you feel utterly relaxed. Visualize every detail. Feel the gentle breeze on your skin, smell the ocean, see the sunset, hear the melody. Remembering these details takes your mind off your worry and helps your body relax.

Sing to yourself. Just the way Dorothy in *The Wizard of Oz* sang. Or make up a silly saying—anything that adds humor or courage to your mental state.

Replace negative self-talk with positive self-talk. Repeat that classic mantra from childhood lore, "I think I can, I think I can, I think I can."

If you often find yourself anxious about exams, try learning yoga, tai chi, or another activity that helps you concentrate without tension. Talk to school counselors or ask a

An exercise class can help you work off test jitters.

sympathetic teacher if you can write a paper or do a project instead of a test.

IT'S ALWAYS SOMETHING

On the original "Saturday Night Live" program, one character's tag line was, "It's always *some*thing." With so much depending on good grades—getting into college, perhaps getting a scholarship, staying out of trouble with your parents—keeping a healthy perspective is a challenge. It helps to remember that like money, grades aren't *every*thing, but like money, they certainly are *some*thing.

First, grades are a nearly universal phenomenon. Unless you are heading off to some remote region in the outback, grades are something with which to grapple. Take heart: in the struggle, you are in good company.

Remember, too, that you can improve your grades. If you can't afford a tutor, ask a teacher or another student for help. Helping you can improve what they learn; as the adage goes, "Teaching others is the best way to learn." Many students form study groups to help each other. Finally, remember that while they do matter, grades are not *all* that matters. Consider the confession of Jenny Hung, an honors student.[8]

IN SEARCH OF EXCELLENCE

In Jenny Hung's first year of high school she took three honors classes because she thought this would help her get into a selective college. The heavy load meant studying almost constantly. As Jenny remembers, "Most days, I would shuffle clumsily from class to class with sleep-clouded eyes and nod off during classroom lectures." One month, she wore sunglasses to school to hide her black-ringed eyes.

For her sacrifices, Jenny reaped the reward of nearly all A's on her report card and saw her name on a poster: Jenny Hung, number-one student, GPA 4.43. This was gratifying, still, Jenny began to question her sacrifices. "Did I want to remember high school as nights without sleep and days of work?" she asked herself. "Sure, it felt good, but it didn't mean much. That I would remain at the top of that list was doubtful, and in the end, the poster was biodegradable. There can be only one valedictorian in each class, and that person usually has to work his fingers to the bone against fierce competition to claim that position. That life," she decided, "was not for me."

The next year Jenny chose fewer honors classes and joined the yearbook staff. She got more sleep and spent more time with friends. "Sometimes I wonder if parents understand what lengths their children go to," said a wiser Jenny, "so that they can sport a bumper sticker proclaiming MY CHILD GOES TO HARVARD!"

As Jenny learned, only you can decide how to balance studying with other activities. And only you can put a healthy perspective on the meaning of grades. John Gatto, a teacher who believes we worry too much about grades, advises that: "Whatever education is, it should make you a unique individual, not a conformist; it should furnish you with an original spirit with which to tackle the big challenges; it should allow you to find values that will be your road map through life; it should make you spiritually rich, a person who loves whatever you are doing, wherever you are, whomever you are with; it should teach you what is important, how to live, and how to die."[9]

CHAPTER 11
Simple Solutions for Improving Your Grades

Since we acknowledge that grades are something, we offer some suggestions for how to get better grades.

GETTING ENOUGH SLEEP

During sleep (and only during the dream state of sleep, actually) your brain builds the networks it needs for memory and learning. During this state, too, it processes and stores what you have learned.

Due to rapid growth and elevated hormones, the average teenager requires 9 to 10 hours of sleep a night. However, teenagers aren't ready to go to sleep early enough to allow for these 9 to 10 hours. Melatonin is a body hormone that causes drowsiness. Teenage bodies tend to produce their melatonin later in the day. So, while adults are starting to feel ready for bed, teens are still going strong.

Here's the problem. While average teenagers need 9 to 10

hours of sleep, they get only 6 to 7 hours on school nights, and often less. Are you a sleep-deprived teenager? Here are three easy ways to tell:

Falling asleep. People who are getting enough sleep generally take between 10 and 20 minutes to fall asleep at night. If you are sleep-deprived, you tend to fall asleep as soon as your head hits the pillow or within a few minutes, or perhaps on the sofa before you even go to bed!

Waking up. People who are getting sufficient sleep can wake in the morning without an alarm clock (unless they need to get up earlier than usual to catch a plane, perhaps). In contrast, sleep-deprived people cannot get up without an alarm clock—and may need several buzzes. When they finally do wake up, they often feel sluggish, as though their bodies were too heavy to move.

Sleeping anywhere. To people getting enough sleep, a warm room or a boring lecture may make them squirm and wish they were anyplace else. To sleep-deprived people, these conditions will make them sleepy, and they may nod off.

If you seem to fit in the sleep-deprived class, use this formula to see *how* sleep-deprived you are.

Step 1: Determine the average number of hours you sleep each school night. If you usually go to bed at 12:30 P.M. and get up at 6 A.M., your average is 5-1/2 hours.

Step 2: Multiply that answer by 5 (5.5 × 5 = 27.5).

Step 3: You probably stay up late one or two school nights a week—studying for an exam, writing a paper, or just watching TV. Estimate how much later you go to bed on those nights and subtract that amount from your total. If you go to bed at

It's hard to stay awake and study when you are sleep-deprived.

2 A.M. two nights a week, then you will subtract 3 hours from 27.5. Your total now is 24.5.

Step 4: Let's say you try to catch up on your sleep weekends, sleeping an extra five hours or so. Add the amount of sleep you get on the weekend to your total. (Friday you went to bed at 2 A.M., slept until noon—that's 10 hours. Saturday night you went to sleep at midnight and got up at 2 P.M. That's a total of 24 hours on the weekend. Not bad, since it is more than you got all week.

So what did you get? 48 hours? Whatever it is, it is probably not close to the 63 to 70 hours a week you need. The difference is why you may have trouble staying alert, or may even fall asleep, in class. About 30 percent of students fall asleep in class at least once a week.[1]

Some schools have tried later starting times. When Edina City schools in suburban Minneapolis moved starting time from 7:25 to 8:30 A.M., the school superintendent, Kenneth Dragseeth, noticed a big difference. "It's been an unqualified success," he said. "There is an alertness and it's not just an alertness in the morning. Students are alert all day."[2]

YOU ARE WHAT YOU EAT

By midmorning, anyone who has skipped breakfast or made do with a sugary snack and a shot of caffeine may find concentrating much more difficult than if he or she had eaten a healthful one.

The dose of refined sugar (the kind that doesn't come from fruit) may wake you up for first period, but by fourth period you will feel hungry and crave more sugar to keep from feeling tired and sluggish. Like caffeine and tobacco, sugar can be addictive. For anyone watching his or her weight, learn the truth: Breakfast is never your enemy and can actually help you. According to a nutritionist from the Cleveland Clinic, a healthful breakfast does not contribute to weight gain. In fact, it fuels the metabolic rate, which becomes sluggish without fuel. And what is healthful? It can be a slice of last night's pizza, hard-boiled eggs, anything to put your body back into full gear, but especially something with protein. Eat a healthful breakfast if you want to learn more and think clearly.

PAYING ATTENTION—TAKING NOTES

The way to pay attention is to be alert. Staying alert in class is the easiest pathway to good grades. And the way to truly stay alert is, again, to get enough sleep.

Two out of five teens report being bored in class[3] and even in the best subjects taught by the most interesting teachers, students pay attention only 65 percent of the time.[4] The traditional way to pay attention is by staying awake and taking notes. Some techniques can help you stay focused—especially if you find yourself getting bored—and take notes as needed. One is to doodle in your notebook. Make doodling a learning experience by sketching or diagramming what the teacher is explaining. Another way is to knit (yes, knit). Doing something mechanical with your hands can help you keep your mind on the lecture. Ask your teachers if they mind if you knit.

Since much of what you will face on tests has been covered in class, it is important to learn to take good notes. One way to make note taking easier is to develop your own shorthand for common words. Ask the teacher if you can tape-record the class so that you can listen to the tape to fill in gaps in your notes. Or check out a book on study skills and learn a new note-taking strategy such as mind mapping. Mind mapping uses diagrams with words or short phrases that sum up an idea. Arranging these words on one sheet will help you remember what you need to know. Our visual memory, which the mind map uses, is stronger than our verbal memory. Most people can recall what they see but have trouble recalling what they hear or even read if it isn't in pictorial form.

If you don't take good notes, ask someone who does to summarize the class for you. This will sharpen that person's memory and help you as well.

MEMORY

Since grades are often based on exams that test your memory of what you have learned, improving your memory will improve your grades. One way to remember material is frequent review. It's helpful to spread out review study over several sessions. In fact, reviewing previous material, studying new material in short spurts, and taking frequent breaks make studying less tedious and can actually improve your memory.

We remember information better if we can relate to it, so creating relationships boosts our memory ability. Try organizing the material into either logical or creative patterns. For example, use time lines to remember dates, sketch trees and fill the branches with material to be learned, create flow charts to show sequences, draw clocks to remember the relationships of items. You can also make outlines of the material or create silly sentences to help you remember dry facts and formulas.

It helps to do memory work just before going to sleep. Sufficient sleep, and the right kind of sleep (REM, or rapid eye movement sleep, which is the state of sleep when we dream), are essential for learning and long-term memory. During sleep, and in particular, during the dream cycle of sleep, our brains make the necessary nerve connections. Interestingly, dreaming is more active after periods of intense studying, such as after studying for finals. Also, during sleep the brain replenishes the neurotransmitters essential to learning and creative thinking.

FREQUENT BREAKS

If you are too antsy to sit and study for long stretches, don't despair. It isn't necessary. Many students have found that taking short breaks (say, 15 minutes) during studying relieves antsiness and helps them stay alert.

CRAMMING

It can happen to even the best students. You didn't have time to finish the reading, you daydreamed too much in class, you weren't ready to study properly. Now it is nine o'clock the night before the exam. All that is left to do is fail—or cram and hope for the best.

Make no mistake; cramming is *not* learning (you probably won't remember much of what you cram after a day or two). Nor is cramming the direct pathway to the honor roll. Cramming is, at best, an emergency measure to keep you from failing, a way to make the most of a bad situation. Here are the basic rules for cramming:

Don't try to learn everything. Choose what you think is the most important material, and skip the rest. One secret for figuring out what is important is to look at the index of your

When desperate, there is nothing else to do but cram.

textbook and study the topics with the most number of entries listed. For example, if your American history text has five entries for the Louisiana Purchase, you can be sure it is important.

If you try to go over all the material, you risk recalling nothing at all. Your time will be spread too thin. So be a warrior and use this formula: Spend a fourth of your time learning new material and the rest drilling yourself in what you have already learned.

Create mind-map review sheets and consolidate what you know onto flash cards. You might add simple illustrations to the review sheets to make it easier to remember the material. Then drill yourself with the flash cards.

Recite the material aloud, and repeat it until you are confident that you can recall it the next day.

Avoid snacking on sugar or overloading on caffeine. Take cues from research on shift work, jet lag, and athletic diets, and eat a protein snack with a carbohydrate—pizza, a hamburger, yogurt and popcorn, whole-grain cereal with milk. These keep you the most alert. A little caffeine—from coffee, colas, and tea—can keep you alert, but a lot can make you jittery and too wired to concentrate.

Try to sit in an upright position, not so comfortably that you will be tempted to doze off. Studying at a desk may keep you more alert than studying in bed.

If you feel drowsy, turn on loud music (using earphones, of course), get a blast of fresh air, try a spurt of exercise, or splash cold water on your face. Remember, the warmer you are, the sleepier you will be. Avoid getting chilled, but keep the room as cool as you can tolerate.

Get some sleep. And remember that memorizing just before sleeping is more effective than trying to learn something when you get up too early. So do your studying before you go to sleep, then get up at your usual hour.

Relax. Cramming is not a great way to retain material, and you are more likely to forget what you have learned if you get nervous. Breathe deeply and try to enjoy the challenge. Do the best that you can and resolve to try harder next time.

A HEALTHY PERSPECTIVE

Learning is fun when you love a subject or enjoy a teacher who makes a subject come alive. However, not all learning is fun. School is where we develop skills in concentration and work on our ability to solve challenging problems. With a good night's sleep, a healthier breakfast, short but frequent study breaks, and the ability to know how to cram when you are really up a creek, you may find improving your grades easier than you thought it could be. And you may find that you learn more and remember what you learn.

CHAPTER 12

Looking on the Bright Side

If you think you can or you think you can't, you're right.

Imagine that you are a four-year-old, sitting in a preschool classroom. The teacher offers you a marshmallow and a choice: If you can wait until she or he returns from a short errand before eating the marshmallow, you will get an extra one. Can you wait?

This choice was presented in a preschool in San Jose, California, to test four-year-olds' ability to delay gratification—to see if they could postpone pleasure for a future goal.[1] Two-thirds of the children waited for the extra marshmallow; the other third ate the snack immediately, choosing instant gratification.

Postponing immediate pleasure requires self-control and perspective; you choose to work hard now for rewards that

Working hard for future goals takes self-control and perspective.

may come later—sometimes years later. A high school senior who wants to be a doctor, for example, must keep studying for eight years or more after the looming exam which is currently leaving no time for sleep, hanging out with friends, or any other activity.

When the San Jose children became teenagers, Walter Mischel, a psychologist at Stanford University, asked their parents to tell him what kind of students these children had become. From their comments, Mischel saw a remarkable difference between the group that had delayed gratification and the group that could not. Those four-year-olds who had demonstrated the patience and self-control to wait for the extra marshmallow could, as teenagers, express themselves more clearly, reason better, concentrate harder, and make plans and follow through with more constancy. In general they showed more eagerness to learn, and had considerably higher SAT scores, as well.

The group who could not wait showed more stubbornness and indecision and had more fights and arguments, many of which they started. As young adults, they appeared to have no more self-control than when they were four-year-olds.[2]

The ability to sacrifice today for future rewards—whether it means doing homework assignments, studying for an exam, or writing a paper when you would rather watch TV or hang out with your friends—is, as author Daniel Goleman explains in his book *Emotional Intelligence*, "the essence of emotional self-regulation." And this regulation, this ability to deny impulse in the service of a goal, gives people the strength to build a business, solve a difficult mathematical equation, or train for a decathlon. It also helps create students who do well, because they can anticipate the fruits of their labor, even if they are in the distant future.

Learning to delay gratification (and become a better student) requires self-control. One way the four-year-olds in the study exercised self-control was to keep busy with other activities. They covered their eyes to not see the temptation, rested their heads in their arms, talked to themselves, sang, played games with their hands and feet. Some tried to sleep. This lesson can be applied to schoolwork. For example, studying in a place where there are fewer distractions makes it easier to focus on studying. Also remembering your goal, perhaps by posting a photograph—a beautiful college campus, an astronaut in space, or a person who delayed gratification and achieved a goal—helps keep the focus on studying.

HIGH HOPES

In another study, C. R. Snyder presented college students at the University of Kansas with this hypothetical situation:[3] You are taking a course in which your goal is to earn a B. The first exam is important, since it will count for nearly a third of your grade. Unfortunately, you do rather poorly on it and receive a D. What are you going to do?

Snyder divided the students into two groups, depending on what they said they would do. In the first group, he put the optimists, the students who expressed high hopes and high expectations of achieving their goals, even with a poor start. The other group, the pessimists, expressed little hope and low expectations for improving the situation.

All the students had similar academic abilities. Thus, at the end of their first semester, they should have had somewhat similar grades. They did not. The optimists had much higher grades than the pessimists. Snyder explained the difference: "Students with high hopes set themselves higher goals and know how to work hard to attain them."[4]

Hope is more than a sunny view that everything will turn out all right. As Snyder defined it, "Hope is believing you have both the will and the way to accomplish your goals, whatever they may be."[5] Or, as Daniel Goleman suggests in *Emotional Intelligence*,[6] people with high hopes know how to motivate themselves and believe that they are resourceful enough to find ways to accomplish their goals. In addition, people with high hopes have the emotional strength to reassure themselves that when they get in a tight spot, things will get better. They believe they will "find a way or make a way."

People with high hopes are flexible enough to see more than one way to reach a goal, or can replace a goal if the first one is unattainable. Perhaps their greatest asset, as students, is their ability to break a formidable task into smaller, manageable pieces.

Those students who know how to break a big term paper into chunks, doing a little at a time until it is complete, have an easier time writing the paper and achieving their goal. Likewise, the students who truly want to learn and do well in school and in life and are hopeful that they will, are more likely to find the creativity and resourcefulness to reach their goals. This reinforces their positive outlook.

LOOKING ON THE BRIGHT SIDE

The quality of optimism can improve your ability to learn, according to Martin Seligman, Ph.D., a researcher from the University of Pennsylvania.[7] Optimism gives rise to hope and, Seligman explains, is the belief that you can have mastery over the events in your life and can meet the challenges that arise. Optimists worry far less than pessimists. They don't spend time worrying about what may never occur. Instead they believe, in general, that eventually things will turn out all right, despite the setbacks and frustrations they may experience.

Optimists tend to believe they can learn from their failures and expect a better outcome the next time around. In contrast, pessimists tend to blame themselves for their failures and doubt that they can change. Thus, optimistic students don't rely on their teachers to validate their ability; nor do they allow a poor grade to destroy their confidence. The pessimists resign themselves to bad grades and tell themselves that it is due to some unfixable flaw: "I'm dumb in math" or "I can't write a sonnet anyway."

Optimism and pessimism become self-fulfilling. The optimist grows more competent, which leads to success, which leads to more confidence. The pessimist continues to give up, frustrated that "the world never seems to cooperate with me."

Some people seem naturally more positive and optimistic than others, and some acquire their pessimism through hard-knock experiences. However, self-efficacy—the belief that one has mastery over the events in one's life and can meet challenges as they come up—can be acquired. Being competent is not a fixed property; you can change your outlook on life.[8]

If you are having trouble improving your grades, remember that you can learn strategies to read better, faster, and more thoroughly. You can learn strategies to study more efficiently. You can improve your writing skills and memory skills, and overcome anxiety about test scores. Most important, you can change your thinking to look on the bright side, to learn from your mistakes and not allow them to defeat you.

GETTING IN THE FLOW

Here's an obvious observation: Students who like to study, study more often and learn more than those students who choose to socialize, watch TV, or do anything else but crack the books. Getting so involved in something, so that you are able to focus and tune out distractions is called being in the "flow," a term coined by psychologist Mihaly Csikszentmihalyi of the University of Chicago. The precise definition of flow is "an automatic, effortless, yet highly focused state of consciousness." Flow can occur when you challenge yourself with a task that you have the skills for but that is neither boring nor *too* much of a challenge. Students who have good study skills and enjoy studying experience the state of flow while studying. You probably have experienced flow in other activities. It's what runners experience when they have a "runner's high" or what artists report as the "standing still of time."

People "in the flow" are unconcerned about how they are doing. They have little thought of success or failure because they are totally caught up in what they are doing.[9] They are intensely involved mentally, but remain relaxed. This relaxation is different from the brain activity of a person who is bored or feels too agitated to concentrate. Someone who is too worried about a grade may spend more time worrying about the exam than studying for it.

One study of flow was conducted at a pilot high school for gifted mathematical students. The students were matched for intelligence and ability.[10] First, the teachers rated the students according to their school performance (not their ability, which was the same for all). Then the students were divided into two groups according to whether they had excellent grades and were high achievers or whether they received mediocre grades (for that school) and were low achievers, whose grades did not reflect their ability.

A remarkable difference was observed between the two groups—remarkable because they had the same potential. Although students in both groups studied far more than average high school students did, the high achievers did nearly twice as much homework and studying as the lower achievers—27 hours a week compared to 15 hours. What were the lower achievers doing while the high achievers were studying? The usual teen activities, including watching TV, surfing the Internet, and socializing.

What proved interesting was how much time students in each group reported being in the flow of studying. High-achieving students reported being in the flow more than twice as often—40 percent of the time compared to only 16 percent of the time for the lower achievers. To repeat, students who do better get in the flow more often, and getting in the flow more easily helps you enjoy learning.

Most people enjoy being in the flow, whether making up rap lyrics, working on a puzzle, or solving a math problem. Time seems to stand still until they check the clock and realize hours, not minutes, have elapsed. So, how can you use flow to improve your grades? The best way is to concentrate on subjects you like. Choose courses where you have some aptitude or some experience. To return to Howard Gardner's theories, students can be highly intelligent in a variety of areas—such as music, art, or understanding human relationships—and these intelligences ought to be as rewarded and cultivated as more traditional ones. So, if music, art, or other less orthodox subjects draw you into the flow, take these courses when you can. Try to do an independent study—perhaps a film—that allows you to work with the material. But remember that even in courses you love, you need to challenge yourself. You'll get bored if things

Being in the flow means being fully absorbed—in solving a problem, learning new material, creating something unique.

are too easy. However, if the work is too challenging, anxiety can prevent you from getting into the flow.

PATIENCE PAYS OFF

When work seems too hard or when you lack confidence, this story of Robert Fritz might keep you going. Fritz started studying the clarinet at the Boston Conservatory of Music.[11] His teacher was a well-known clarinetist, Attilio Poto.

Poto's first assignment was difficult and even after a week of practice, Fritz could not play it well. Yet at the next lesson, Poto assigned him a more difficult piece and each following week, a progressively harder piece. Each week Fritz was unable to master the piece.

At the sixth lesson Poto had Fritz play the first piece of music, which Fritz had not practiced since the week it was assigned. To Fritz's delight, he could easily play it. Next he found he could play the second week's exercise, too.

Just as trying a new exercise or warming up for a sport you haven't played in a while causes sore muscles, stretching your mind may cause you pain. But, with persistence, this stretching can lead to accomplishments you thought you could never make—and to excellence as well.

THE THOUSAND-BIRD THEORY OF LEARNING

Sri Chinmoy, an Indian yogi master, decided to paint 100,000 birds. (Remember this, we'll get back to it.) Wang Yani, an artist from China, displayed a natural talent for painting at the age of three. After a year of painting cats, she started painting monkeys.[12] At first her monkeys looked more like cats than monkeys, but in time, they began to resemble monkeys. When she was ten, her monkey paintings were exquisite works. There is an important lesson here: Terkel's Thousand-Bird Theory of Learning Anything. If you don't know how to paint or know nothing about birds, and paint 1,000 birds, or better yet, 10,000, or (like Sri Chinmoy) 100,000, you will learn something about both painting and birds. This is a certainty. And during the learning process, it is essential to ignore your critics, forget about grades, and be passionate about learning. This is how you will be able to achieve the state of flow. You may also gain feelings of optimism and self-esteem. For it is through mastering what we think we cannot do that we develop self-esteem. And it is through such experiences that we live our lives fully.

CHAPTER 13

Sink or Swim: The Race for College

Sadie was getting such poor grades and spending so much time daydreaming in class that her high school counselor suggested she consider a vocation that did not require a college education. Then a family friend began to tutor her, and Sadie's attitude toward school began to change. With a weak record, she didn't dream of applying to a selective college. Instead, Sadie chose to attend Santa Rosa Community College, a two-year school with a policy of accepting all students. Santa Rosa has a program to help students adapt to college and prepares them to transfer to four-year colleges and universities.

Santa Rosa was a good choice. Sadie's confidence in studying and her interest in learning grew, due to excellent teachers and her increased maturity. She learned to write better, to read with greater understanding, to reason more clearly. She gained an appreciation for subjects such as art history and anthropology, subjects she never knew could be so fascinating or important.

In time, Sadie grew restless and moved to New York City. After working for a year as a nanny and a waitress, she applied to a small liberal-arts school in the city, Eugene Lang College at The New School University. With small classes, passionate faculty, and lively classroom discussions, Eugene Lang challenged her. After a year, Sadie applied to Columbia University, a highly competitive school. By now, the grades on Sadie's college transcript reflected her passion for learning.

At Columbia, Sadie first proved herself in the university's College of General Studies and was then admitted to the regular program. She continued working hard, now motivated by a love of what she was learning. She liked her professors, the course reading, the assignments, and her classmates. At age twenty-five, after a long and circuitous route, Sadie graduated from Columbia University with honors, a nearly perfect GPA, and a thirst for learning.

After graduation she worked at a nonprofit organization and made plans to go to law school. Would anyone who knew Sadie in her teen years have guessed her future? Certainly not her teachers, her guidance counselor, her classmates, or even at times, Sadie herself. The purpose of telling you this true story is to inspire you to do the best you can without going through high school sleep-deprived, full of anxiety, and believing that life is all downhill if you don't get into a selective college.

For every Sadie, there is also a Matthew, who took a challenging course load all through high school and scored over 1450 in his SATs, including a perfect math score. He was president of his school's political action club, a drum major in the band, and the religious director of his youth group. He was even a published poet. Despite his record, Matthew was turned down by the many selective schools to which he applied. Only the least selective school accepted him. Matthew can get an excellent education at this school; and because he is self-motivated and enjoys learning, he probably will.

Matthew's story is not a rationalization for not working hard in high school. Nor should students let rejections undermine their confidence. There are too many able and hardworking students like Matthew, and not enough places in the first-year classes of selective schools. As an example, in 1999, Tufts University in Massachusetts rejected a third of its valedictorian-applicants, and a number of applicants with perfect SAT scores. Why? Simple arithmetic—13,500 students competed for 1,200 spots in the class.[1]

Fortunately, most colleges and universities in the United States do not require all A's or even B's; only transcripts that demonstrate the ability to do average or better work. Some schools simply require a high school diploma. In Ohio, for example, eight state universities have open-admissions policies and accept all applicants. Even the most competitive schools accept students who have never received grades, as well as transfer students like Sadie, who have proved themselves in junior colleges and elsewhere. Remember, too, that college is only one road to take. Many technical institutions, such as computer schools, offer associate degree programs. Other options include trade schools, such as culinary institutes, where students learn to be chefs and caterers; graphic arts programs; and fashion institutes. And some careers—and lifestyles—require no advanced degrees.

Clearly, in college admissions, grades count and count a

great deal. The question critics ask is: Should they? Alfie Kohn argues that high schools should be in the business of teaching, not sorting students out for college admissions officers. Even when the process (college admissions and its reliance on grades) doesn't seem to have its priorities straight, high schools don't have to be dragged down to that level.[2]

WORKING FOR THE GRADE

Michele Fernandez worked as an admissions officer at Dartmouth College and later described the selection process of selective schools in *A Is for Admission*.[3] If you want a selective school, she advises you to take challenging courses as early as you can, even in eighth grade. Strive to do well. Also remember that teachers will be asked to comment on your personality and character. According to her experience, the worst comment a teacher can make, one that will surely undermine the chance of an acceptance, is to describe someone as a grade grubber, uninterested in learning for learning's sake but working just to get good grades.

Most important, Fernandez suggests asking yourself if you honestly want to go to a selective school, and why. Take a good look at yourself and your motivation; ask yourself why you are working so hard for A's. "Is it because your parents are forcing you to do hours of homework when you'd be happier shooting hoops in the driveway? Do you dread the thought of plowing through novels for your English class? Do you see your classes and even school as a stepping-stone to success?"[4] Fernandez advises you not to choose a school simply so that you can display its diploma. "Such educations are expensive and difficult," she explains. "You might be better served at schools that make fewer academic demands, both in high school in preparation for them, and at them."[5] Seeing the highly selective schools as offering the only pathway to success in life is incorrect and blinds students to the value of all their other choices.

WHAT IS WRONG WITH THE PICTURE?

Is it fair that admissions are based so much on grades and SAT scores? After all, A's are not always the sign of the most able or dedicated student, nor are high SAT scores a sure indication of superior intelligence. Harvard's former president Derek Bok, and Princeton's former president William G. Bowen studied the records of thousands of minority students

With the advantage of a year or two of college behind them, the staff members of the Harvard Lampoon, a humor magazine, poke fun at high school students' anxiety about gaining admission to the perfect college.

who were admitted to selective colleges in 1976, although their grades and SAT scores did not generally meet the school's criteria.

Bok and Bowen found that success for these students after college had no relation to their grades or SATs. What their findings imply, argue Bok and Bowen, is that admission should not be based on grades and SAT scores alone. Admissions officers should view students as individuals (what the school can do for a particular student) and collectively (accepting students with diverse backgrounds). "Admissions should be fair," they wrote in their book, *The Shape of the River*, "but fairness does not mean that only grades and SAT scores should count or that high grades 'earn' you the right to acceptance over someone with lower grades. That right is not possessed by anyone."[6] In their opinion, a diversified student body, including some students who don't have high grades and who bring other skills and talents, and diversity, offers everyone—including the rest of society—a richer education and college experience.

Bowen and Bok also stress that A students with very high SAT scores are not necessarily the most able. Grades and board scores often reflect advantages such as expensive tutoring, exposure to better teaching and smaller classes at privileged private and public schools, a stable family life (valedictorians, for example, overwhelmingly come from intact, two-parent families), and other factors. Do such advantages deserve to be rewarded? Should students who lack access to them be at a disadvantage? Most important, while individual students may benefit, overall, society suffers from discrimination when it denies otherwise promising individuals the chance to compete on a level academic playing field.

For better or worse, grades and college acceptance are closely related. Poor grades almost certainly guarantee rejection at the most selective schools. Good grades do not guarantee admission to these schools. But remember, despite their reputations, these schools do not guarantee that graduates will learn more or find interesting jobs or be happy. They offer stimulating courses, great libraries, excellent resources, and a student body from all over the world—many of whom are bright, talented, and earnest about learning. However, less selective schools can offer a fine education and other important advantages: small classes, support and personal attention, and greater access to faculty. And if grades are unimportant, but learning is, you might consider an ungraded college.

If a selective school is what you want, then working hard to get there may be worth your while. However, you may decide it isn't for you. Then perhaps, as Fernandez suggests, "Save the struggle for graduate school or spare yourself altogether."[7] With less pressure during high school, you can get an interesting after-school job or pursue a talent, and if nothing else, get enough sleep so that you get more out of your high school education and can manage your workload.

CHAPTER 14
Grades Aren't Everything

Good grades can get you into a good school. Good schools can get you good jobs. Good jobs can get you the "good life." And so it goes. Good grades = the only ticket to success. This is the prevailing theory, but it doesn't hold up. Without good grades you can become president of the United States, CEO of a major multinational company, or a wildly successful writer. And you'll be in great company.

Albert Einstein, a brilliant scientist, nearly flunked out of school at fifteen. Liz Claiborne, the founder of a multinational company, never finished high school. Ronald Reagan was twice elected United States president, although he was an average student at an average college. As these successful people demonstrate, a person can succeed without good grades.

Nor do good grades, even the highest grades, guarantee success. Karen Arnold, a professor at Radcliffe College, studied 81 high school valedictorians. She found that while they

Albert Einstein, who succeeded after nearly flunking out of school

earned high marks in college, few reached the pinnacle of success in their careers, and four never completed college. "They're not mold-breakers," explained Arnold. A few among the valedictorians were brilliant, but most, she found, were just students who worked hard, stayed focused on their studies, and followed the rules.[1]

WORK AND GRADES

Some job applications ask for your college grade point average. This happens most often in computer science, engineering, accounting, or other fields where number crunching matters. But many companies don't care about your grades or class rank. Hershey Lerner, founder and CEO of a multi-million-dollar packaging company says he doesn't "give a hoot" about a person's grades. He likes to hire people who weren't such great students. "They are more likely to think for themselves," he observes. "I want people who can take calculated risks."[2]

The secret is out of the bag. With mediocre grades you can be a success, even a millionaire. If you are going into business for yourself, which is how many millionaires build their fortunes, you don't have to have top grades, or a college diploma. Banks don't ask for your GPA; neither does your accountant or your customers.

Thomas J. Stanley, a business professor, is the author of the best-selling book, *The Millionaire Mind*. (Apparently many people are curious about millionaires and how to become one.) Stanley surveyed hundreds of millionaires. Many had been B or C students. Nor did these millionaires credit their success to being smart. Most believed that the keys to their success were honesty and discipline, being able to get along with people, having a supportive spouse, and working hard at work they loved. "If you perform well in your chosen vocation," Stanley states, "you are likely to earn more than others, especially if you are self-employed."

Millionaires also know how to accumulate greater wealth, mostly by "having the common sense to save and invest."[3] They have creativity and what Hershey Lerner was looking for—the willingness and wisdom to know how to take calculated risks. But remember that many professions—including teaching, social work, the ministry, and others—offer intangible, non-monetary rewards.

SUCCESS IN LIFE

Perhaps the most important lesson is not about whether grades do or don't count, but a caution to avoid mistaking grades for learning—and to not miss out on learning because you are worried about the grade. Success often comes to those with intense curiosity, a voracious reading habit, a passion for learning new ideas and skills for their own sake, and especially to those who make learning a lifetime pursuit.

Ralph Waldo Emerson, a philosopher who lived during a time when grades didn't matter so much, offers some sage musings about success.

> *Success is to laugh often and much, to win the respect of intelligent people and affection of children, to earn the appreciation of honest critics and endure the betrayal of false friends, to appreciate beauty, to find the best in others, to leave the world a better place, whether by a healthy child, a garden patch, or a redeemed social condition, to know one life has breathed easier because you have lived. This is to have succeeded.*

As these wise words remind us, grades aren't everything.

Notes

INTRODUCTION

1. Ohmer Milton, Howard R. Pollio, and James A. Eison, *Making Sense of College Grades* (San Francisco: Jossey-Bass, 1986). p. 3.

2. Alfie Kohn, *Punished by Rewards* (Boston: Houghton Mifflin Co., 1993), p. 12.

CHAPTER 1

1. Mark W. Durm, "An A Is Not an A: A History of Grading," *Educational Forum* (Spring 1993), p. 295.

2. Carol Sager, *Eliminating Grades in Schools: An Allegory for Change* (Milwaukee: ASQC Quality Press, 1995), p. 1.

CHAPTER 2

1. Ohmer Milton, Howard R. Pollio, and James A. Eison, *Making Sense of College Grades* (San Francisco: Jossey-Bass, 1986), p. 11.

2. Robert Lynn Canady and Phyllis Riley Hotchkiss, "It's a Good Score! Just a Bad Grade," *Phi Delta Kappan* (September 1989), p. 69.

3. *Ibid.*, p. 69.

4. E. Ray Dockery, "How to Improve Grading Practices," *Teaching for Excellence* (September 1994).

5. Milton, Pollio, and Eison, *Making Sense of College Grades*, pp. 166, 169.

CHAPTER 3

1. Howard Kirschenbaum, Rodney Napier, and Sidney Simon, *Wad-Ja-Get? The Grading Game in American Education* (New York: Hart, 1971), pp. 99–101.

2. Kirschenbaum, Napier, and Simon, *Wad-Ja-Get?* p. 56.

3. E. Ray Dockery, "How to Improve Grading Practices," *Teaching for Excellence* (September 1994), p. 40.

4. Robert Lynn Canady, "Teacher Behaviors Which May Vary Depending on Whether We Focus Primarily on Sorting and Selecting or Teaching and Learning." Informational packet.

5. Robert Lynn Canady and Phyllis Riley Hotchkiss, "It's a Good Score! Just a Bad Grade," *Phi Delta Kappan* (September 1989), p. 69.

6. Robert Lynn Canady, "The Problem with Averaging a Zero in Determining a Valid Summative Grade." Informational packet.

7. Dockery, "How to Improve Grading Practices," p. 45.

8. Toronto District School Board, "Questions and Answers: Assessment, Evaluation and Reporting" from the Ministry of Education (August 11, 1999), *http://www.tdsb.on.ca/ssr/FAQs/METassmt/AssAns3.htm*.

9. Margot A. Olson, "Should BAD Behavior Mean BAD Grades?" *Virginia Journal of Education* (April 1991), p. 12.

CHAPTER 4

1. Ohmer Milton, Howard R. Pollio, and James A. Eison, *Making Sense of College Grades* (San Francisco: Jossey-Bass, 1986), pp. 142, 148.

2. Alfie Kohn, *Punished by Rewards* (Boston: Houghton Mifflin Co., 1993), pp. 17, 67.

3. *Ibid.*, p. 11.

4. Alfie Kohn, "From Degrading to De-Grading," *The High School Magazine* (March 1999), p. 40.

5. Thomas Armstrong, *7 Kinds of Smart: Identifying and Developing Your Multiple Intelligences* (New York: Plume, 1999), p. 8.

6. Howard Gardner, *Multiple Intelligences: The Theory in Practice (*New York: Basic Books, 1993) pp. 6–10.

7. Armstrong, *7 Kinds of Smart*, p. 224.

8. Gardner, *Multiple Intelligences*, pp. 13–15.

CHAPTER 5

1. Jerry Mintz, "Summerhill Wins in Court!" *The Education Revolution* (Spring 2000).

2. Interview with Jerry Mintz, director of Alternative Education Resource Organization (AERO).

CHAPTER 6

1. Alfie Kohn, "From Degrading to De-grading," *The High School Magazine* (March 1999), p. 41.

2. *People* (July 12, 1999), p. 74.

3. Nicholas Lemann, *The Big Test: The Secret History of the American Meritocracy* (New York: Farrar, Straus and Giroux, 2000).

4. Kohn, "From Grading to De-grading," p. 41.

5. Michele Feutsch, "Is Failure a Path to Success?" *The* [Cleveland] *Plain Dealer* (April 9, 2000), p. 10A.

6. Carolyn Kleiner and Mary Lord, "The Cheating Game," *U.S. News & World Report* (Nov. 11, 1999), pp. 54–65.

7. Ohmer Milton, Howard Pollio, and James A. Eison, *Making Sense of College Grades* (San Francisco: Jossey-Bass, 1986), p. 214.

8. *Ibid.*, p. 219.

9. John Gatto, *Dumbing Us Down* (Philadelphia: New Society, 1992), p. 84.

10. Alfie Kohn, *No Contest* (New York: Houghton Mifflin, 1992), p. 46.

11. David Johnson and Robert Johnson reviewed studies of classroom competition and found evidence that it fails to improve learning but that cooperation does. Cited in Kohn, "From Degrading to De-grading," p. 48.

12. UCLA Higher Education Research Institute, reported in Ben Wildavsky, "At Least They Have High Self-esteem," *U.S. News & World Report* (Feb. 7, 2000), p. 50.

13. *Ibid.*, p. 50.

CHAPTER 7

1. Bob Corbett, *The Cheater's Handbook: The Naughty Student's Bible* (New York: HarperCollins, 1999).

2. *Who's Who Among American High School Students* selects 5 percent of the nation's 14 million high school students for their achievements and their community work.

3. Carolyn Kleiner and Mary Lord, "The Cheating Game," *U.S. News & World Report* (Nov. 11, 1999), p. 54

4. *Ibid.*, p. 60.

5. *Ibid.*, p. 54.

6. *Ibid.*, p. 55.

7. *Ibid.*, p. 55.

8. *Ibid.*, p. 55.

9. *Ibid.*, pp. 54–63.

10. Interview with Chris Sperry, April 27, 2000, via mail.

CHAPTER 8

1. Alfie Kohn, "From Degrading to De-Grading," *The High School Magazine* (March 1999), p. 42.

2. *Ibid.*, p. 42.

3. "Teens Don't Rush to Give Their School Highest Grades: Only One in

Five Rates an 'A,'" *Youthviews: The Newsletter of the Gallup Youth Survey* (Jan. 2000), p. 5.

4. Kohn, "From Degrading to De-grading," p. 40.

5. Howard Kirschenbaum, Rodney Napier, and Sidney Simon, *Wad-Ja-Get? The Grading Game in American Education* (New York: Hart, 1971), p. 103.

6. Ohmer Milton, Howard Pollio, and James A. Eison, *Making Sense of College Grades* (San Francisco: Jossey-Bass, 1986), p. 71.

7. Carol Sager, *Eliminating Grades in Schools: An Allegory for Change* (Milwaukee: ASQC Quality Press, 1995), p. 51.

8. Kohn, "From Degrading to De-grading," p. 46.

CHAPTER 9

1. John Caniglia, "Cheerleader Drops Suit Against District," *The* [Cleveland] *Plain Dealer* (Jan. 27, 2000), p. 1B.

2. Paula Sullivan, "Let Those Who Can, Teach," *Wall Street Journal* (April 28, 1998).

CHAPTER 10

1. "Foundation for Learning: Parents vs. Bad Grades," *Youthviews* (January 1994), p. 3.

2. Howard Pollio, Lee Humphreys, and James A. Eison, "Patterns of Parental Reaction to Student Grades," *Higher Education* (Issue 22, 1991), pp. 31–42.

3. *Ibid.*, p. 41.

4. *Ibid.*, p. 97.

5. *Ibid.*, p. 97.

6. Ben Wildavsky, "At Least They Have High Self-esteem," *U.S. News & World Report* (Feb. 7, 2000), p. 50.

7. *Ibid.*, p. 50.

8. Jenny Hung, "Surviving a Year of Sleepless Nights," *Newsweek* (Sept. 20, 1999), p. 9.

9. John Gatto, *Dumbing Us Down* (Philadelphia: New Society, 1992), p. 75.

CHAPTER 11

1. James B. Maas, Ph.D., *Power Sleep* (New York: Random House, 1998), p. 7.

2. Catherine Gilfether, "Too Sleepy for School," *The* [Cleveland] *Plain Dealer* (April 12, 1997), pp. 1, 7.

3. Ben Wildavsky, "At Least They Have High Self-esteem," *U.S. News & World Report* (Feb. 7, 2000), p. 50.

4. Ohmer Milton, Howard Pollio, and James Eison, *Making Sense of College Grades* (San Francisco: Jossey-Bass, 1986), p. 170.

CHAPTER 12

1. Yuichi Shoda, Walter Mischel, and Philip K. Peake, "Predicting Adolescent Cognitive and Self-regulatory Competencies from Preschool Delay of Gratification," *Developmental Psychology* (1990), pp. 978–986; reported in Daniel Goleman, *Emotional Intelligence* (New York: Bantam Books, 1995), pp. 81–83.

2. *Ibid.*, pp. 80–85.

3. C. R. Snyder et al., "The Will and the Ways: Development and Validation of an Individual-Differences Measure of Hope," *Journal of Personality and Social Psychology* volume 60, p. 4 (1991), reported in Goleman, *Emotional Intelligence*, pp. 86–87.

4. *Ibid.*

5. Daniel Goleman, *Emotional Intelligence* (New York: Bantam Books, 1997), p. 83.

6. *Ibid.*, p. 87.

7. Interview of Martin Seligman by Daniel Goleman, *The New York Times* (February 3, 1987).

8. To learn more about optimism, read Martin Seligman, Ph.D., *Learned Optimism* (New York: Alfred Knopf, 1991).

9. Goleman, *Emotional Intelligence*, p. 90.

10. Jeanne Nakamura, "Optimal Experience and the Uses of Talent," in Mihaly Csikszentmihalyi and Isabella Csikszentmihalyi, *Optimal Experience: Psychological Studies in Flow in Consciousness* (Cambridge: Cambridge University Press, 1988), reported in Goleman, *Emotional Intelligence*, p. 93.

11. Robert Fritz, *The Path of Least Resistance: Learning to Become the Creative Force in Your Own Life* (New York: Fawcett Columbine, 1989), pp. 201–202.

12. Chen-sun Cheng, *A Young Painter: The Life and Painting of Wang Yani* (New York: Scholastic, 1991).

CHAPTER 13

1. Ethan Bronner, "For '99 College Applicants, Stiffest Competition Ever," *The New York Times* (June 12, 1999), pp. 1, 11.

2. Alfie Kohn, "From Degrading to De-grading," *The High School Magazine* (March 1999), p. 41.

3. Michele Fernandez, *A Is for Admission* (New York: Warner Books, 1997).

4. *Ibid.*, p. 18.

5. *Ibid.*, p. 19.

6. William G. Bowen and Derek Bok, *The Shape of the River* (Princeton: Princeton University Press, 1998), p. 277.

7. Fernandez, *A Is for Admission*, p. 18.

CHAPTER 14

1. Marilyn Gardner, "Study Tracks Success of High School Valedictorians," *Christian Science Monitor* (May 25, 1995), p. 12. Karen Arnold published her findings in *Lives of Promise: What Becomes of High School Valedictorians?* (San Francisco: Jossey-Bass, 1995).

2. Interview with Hershey Lerner, May 1, 2000, Hudson, Ohio.

3. Thomas J. Stanley, Ph.D., *The Millionaire Mind* (Kansas City: Andrews McMeel Publishing, 2000), p. 71.

Glossary

aptitude: how ready and able a person is to learn

assessment: a formal evaluation of a student's academic performance

average: a measure of central tendency; a summary of a student's grades in a class or in total; in the middle, neither high nor low in ranking

class rank: how a student's grade point average compares to other students' in a graduating class. Can be stated as an absolute number (student 260) or as part of a statistical percentage (top 10 percent).

cooperative learning: learning in a group, with members helping each other. If students are graded, all members of the group receive the same grade for the assignment.

cramming: studying for a test at the last minute. Cramming generally results in the use of short-term recall during the test rather than learning the material.

curve, grading on the: inflating or deflating students' scores on an exam in order to have the distribution of scores match an arbitrary bell-shaped curve distribution (few high and low grades, with most grades falling in the middle)

delayed gratification: when the reward comes long after the behavior

deschooling: an educational philosophy that criticizes rigid curricula and conventional ways of teaching in favor of more informal methods that encourage independence, creativity, and critical thinking

extrinsic motivation: when a person does something for someone else, or to receive a reward or avoid a punishment

flow: a state of mind where a person is totally absorbed in a task; the mind is active but relaxed

free school: a democratic school that emphasizes freedom and equality. Classes are optional and students are not graded.

general equivalency diploma (GED): a formal document issued by the state department of education or another authorized agency certifying that an individual has met state requirements for high school graduation by attaining satisfactory scores on the state-specified exam

grade: individual or cumulative score of a student's academic performance; level of education, such as 9th grade

grade inflation: an artificial rise of average student grades

grade point: the numerical equivalent for a letter grade, used in determining grade point average; generally, an A = 4, B = 3, C = 2, D = 1, and F = 0.

grade point average (GPA): the result of averaging numerical grades together to get an overview of a student's achievement for a semester, year, or school career

honor roll: a list of students who have earned a set GPA for a marking period, year, or school career

honor society: an association that offers membership to students who have achieved high academic standing and, frequently, fulfilled requirements for distinction in leadership or citizenship

intrinsic motivation: when people do something for themselves, because they enjoy or value the task or the satisfaction of accomplishing the task

Ivy League, the: the eight East Coast universities (Brown, Columbia, Cornell, Dartmouth, Harvard, University of Pennsylvania, Princeton, and Yale) that are among the nation's oldest, and among its most selective.

meditation: an approach to achieve relaxation and mental neutrality; its benefits are reported to include reduced stress and improved educational performance

Merit Scholarships: financial awards given to college-bound students, based on academic performance and standardized test scores

meritocracy: a society in which excellence is cultivated and rewarded to create a superior ruling class that governs with insight, wisdom, and knowledge. Social standing and wealth are disregarded in the choices of leaders.

mind mapping: a system of note taking that uses single words and short phrases to organize facts and ideas in a way that makes them easy to understand, memorize, and recall

motivation: a psychological term that refers to internal or external factors that activate or maintain an individual's behavior

multiple-choice test: a test that requires the test taker to choose the correct or best answer from several options

multiple intelligence theory: a theory proposed by Howard Gardner that challenges traditional notions of intelligence (IQ) by labeling a number of areas that people excel in as intelligences. In multiple intelligence theory, body awareness, musical talent, spacial understanding, and other traits are as valued as verbal and mathematical skills.

objectivity: when decisions are made based on facts rather than opinion

optimism: a positive outlook; believing that the best is possible

pessimism: a negative outlook; believing that the best is often not possible

portfolio: a collection of a student's work over a period of time

sleep deprivation: a condition resulting from extended periods of inadequate sleep

subjective: when personal views are brought into the decision-making process

ungraded schools: schools that do not use letter or number grades to symbolize achievement; schools that do not sort students by grade levels; also called nongraded schools

valedictorian: the student with the highest GPA in a graduating class; frequently selected to speak at the graduation ceremony

Selected Bibliography

Bowen, William G. and Derek Bok. *The Shape of the River*. Princeton: Princeton University Press, 1998. (An argument for affirmative action.)

Buzan, Tony and Barry Buzan. *The Mind Map Book*. New York: Dutton, 1993.

Fritz, Robert. *The Path of Least Resistance*. New York: Fawcett Columbine, 1989. (An insightful look at creativity.)

Gardner, Howard. *The Unschooled Mind*. New York: Basic Books, 1991. (By the psychologist who developed the theory of multiple intelligences.)

Gatto, John. *Dumbing Us Down*. Philadelphia: New Society, 1992. (A passionate essay calling for school reform.)

Goleman, Daniel. *Emotional Intelligence*. New York: Bantam Books, 1997. (Fascinating research on predicting success in school.)

Gurvis, Sandra. *Careers for Non-Conformists*. New York: Marlowe & Co., 2000. (Career choices that don't depend on high school grades.)

Hern, Matt, ed. *Deschooling Our Lives.* Philadelphia: New Society Press, 1996. (Essays on alternative education.)

Hernandez, Michele A. *A Is for Admission.* New York: Warner Books, 1997. (The author reveals what she learned working in admissions at Dartmouth.)

Kirshenbaum, Howard, Rodney Napier, and Sidney Simon. *Wad-Ja-Get? The Grading Game in American Education.* New York: Hart Publishing, 1971. (A look at grade reform in the 1960s.)

Kohn, Alfie. *No Contest.* New York: Houghton Mifflin, 1992. (The arguments against competition.)

———*Punished by Rewards.* New York: Houghton Mifflin, 1993. (A dense yet thought provoking discussion of how rewards suppress motivation.)

Lemann, Nicholas. *The Big Test: The Secret History of the American Meritocracy.* New York: Farrar, Straus and Giroux, 1999. (A well-documented history of meritocracy in higher education.)

Maas, James B. *Power Sleep.* New York: Villard, 1998. (Everything you ever needed to know about sleep.)

Marzano, Robert J. *Transforming Classroom Grading.* Alexandria, VA: Association for Supervision and Curriculum Development, 2000. (A well-researched argument for reforming grading practices in public schools.)

Milton, Ohmer, Howard Pollio, and James Eison. *Making Sense of College Grades.* San Francisco: Jossey-Bass, 1986. (A more academic book about the relationships among grades, college performance, and careers.)

Nathan, Amy. *Surviving Homework.* Brookfield, CT: The Millbrook Press, 1996. (Tips for making homework easier.)

Robinson, Amy. *What Smart Students Know.* New York: Three Rivers Press, 1993. (Study tips by a successful tutor.)

Sager, Carol. *Eliminating Grades in Schools.* Milwaukee: ASQC Quality Press, 1995. (An argument for abolishing grading in the classroom.)

Seligman, Martin. *Learned Optimism.* New York: Knopf, 1991. (A book about optimism.)

Stanley, Thomas J. *The Millionaire Mind.* Kansas City: Andrews McMeel Publishing, 2000. (Why grades aren't everything.)

Index

Page numbers in *Italics* indicate illustrations.

About the Authors

Amy Ford

Marni Terkel is a recent graduate of Hampshire College, where she studied the effects of social inequalities. As an alternative to grades, Hampshire appraises students' achievement through faculty evaluations and portfolios. This experience was one of the factors that inspired *What's an "A" Anyway?*

Marni Terkel has tutored, worked with children in battered women's shelters, and is now teaching at a progressive preschool.

Alan Doe

Susan Neiburg Terkel writes to bring clarity and understanding to difficult contemporary issues, including sexual ethics, abortion, child custody, non-violence, and drug policy. Ms. Terkel was consulting editor for *The Encyclopedia of Ethics*, is the founder and director of the Institute for Ethics in Education, and is preparing an ethics curriculum for high school students. She earned a degree in child development and family relationships at Cornell University.